Ethics of Big Data

Kord Davis
with Doug Patterson

O'REILLY®

Beijing · Cambridge · Farnham · Köln · Sebastopol · Tokyo

Ethics of Big Data

by Kord Davis with Doug Patterson

Published by O'Reilly Media, Inc., 1005 Gravenstein Highway North, Sebastopol, CA 95472.

O'Reilly books may be purchased for educational, business, or sales promotional use. Online editions are also available for most titles (*http://my.safaribooksonline.com*). For more information, contact our corporate/institutional sales department: 800-998-9938 or *corporate@oreilly.com*.

Editors: Julie Steele and Courtney Nash	**Production Editor:** Kristen Borg
	Cover Designer: Karen Montgomery
	Interior Designer: David Futato
	Illustrator: Rebecca Demarest

Revision History for the First Edition:

2012-09-13   First release

See *http://oreilly.com/catalog/errata.csp?isbn=9781449311797* for release details.

ISBN: 978-1-449-31179-7

[LSI]

To my friends and family. Who make it possible.

Table of Contents

Preface

Philosophy and business don't always get along well. Philosophy is generally not much concerned with the practical implications of its investigations and, conversely, business is often deeply interested in the tactical outcomes of its operations.

And ethics is a loaded word. Preconceived notions of what ethics mean, even as a legitimate field of study, often make people shy away from it as a topic of discussion. It's hard to talk about what we don't fully understand and even the word itself can sometimes imply judgment: do-this-don't-do-that kinds of directives and obligations. And we all frequently chafe when we think we're being told what to do.

This book tries to diminish these difficulties. Not because they are difficult (ethical inquiry can be hard work) but because they create barriers to helping organizations benefit from philosophical thinking and inquiry. And there are plenty of benefits. The primary characteristic of my approach was to recognize that business contexts, markets, companies, cultures, geographic distinctions, and organizational size and maturity all contribute to an unwieldy set of complex and different circumstances. Circumstances with which you are much more familiar in your own case and therefore more qualified to determine how best to inform your organization's operations with ethical inquiry.

People often ask me: "how did you get from a degree in philosophy to consulting?" The answer varied and evolved over the years—mostly as consequence of me learning more about how to answer the question. And it bears on the relationship between philosophy and business in general and ethics and big data in particular.

My interest in technology started in 5th grade when my grandmother gave me a 75 in One Electronic Project Kit—vintage editions are still available on eBay! It turned out that wires and batteries and capacitors and resistors could all be combined and recombined to create brand new circuits that performed all manner of fascinating and interesting functions. Through high school programming classes and working in telecommunications as a Radioman for most of my nearly 5 years in the United States Coast Guard, I came to realize that what was engaging about technology was that it spoke to the essence of some important and hard facts about our physical world. Energy flowed and could be directed. Radio waves were generated and could carry digital information. Transistors and other semiconductor materials could be combined to create powerful new computing processing and storage devices. And software could be written that would make all those devices do some amazing things.

You'd think I would have studied physics or computer science. Instead what happened is that philosophy captured my attention by offering the best of both worlds: the rigor of analysis and investigation into the essence of all things and an open and willing approach to understanding how science and technology itself works. I was sold.

A key motivation for this book is to apply the tools that philosophy in general, and ethical inquiry in particular, provide us to evolve technology and shape it into tools that can help us live better, easier lives.

Enter big data. This aspect of technology is unique in that its very nature (its essence) is to create, connect, correlate, aggregate, store, process, and report on massive amounts of information. As human beings, we have simply never seen, let alone understood, how to manage that much data. One of the implications of amassing this much information, especially about people and their behaviors, is what I'm calling big data's "forcing function." It is pushing us—whether we like it or not—to consider serious ethical issues including whether certain uses of big data violate fundamental civil, social, political, and legal rights.

These are long, complex, and deeply important conversations. And, as a society, we're not having enough of them. But it's hard to have them because we're not accustomed to having them in business environments very much. And ethics can be a loaded word. So, the hope is that this work will help you and your organization begin to develop the capability to engage in explicit ethical inquiry in new ways and in new contexts. To begin, the methods, concepts, and intentional vocabulary in this book are intended to provide you with a better ability to determine, in your own unique circumstances, how best to execute on and utilize the results of explicit ethical inquiry to improve your organization.

Such discussions are in their infancy in terms of understanding both the issues and their outcomes. We are all just figuring it out as we go—a circumstance about which we have no other choice. Nobody in history has ever had the opportunity to innovate, or been faced with the risks of unintended consequences, that big data now provides.

I look forward to being a part of that ongoing discussion. O'Reilly has constructed a tool chain that allows this book to be easily updated and re-distributed through print-on-demand and digital channels. As the collective understanding and use of big data evolves, the work can evolve right along with it.

Conventions Used in This Book

The following typographical conventions are used in this book:

Italic

Indicates new terms, URLs, email addresses, filenames, and file extensions.

Using Code Examples

This book is here to help you get your job done. In general, you may use the code in this book in your programs and documentation. You do not need to contact us for permission unless you're reproducing a significant portion of the code. For example, writing a program that uses several chunks of code from this book does not require permission. Selling or distributing a CD-ROM of examples from O'Reilly books does require permission. Answering a question by citing this book and quoting example code does not require permission. Incorporating a significant amount of example code from this book into your product's documentation does require permission.

We appreciate, but do not require, attribution. An attribution usually includes the title, author, publisher, and ISBN. For example: "*Ethics of Big Data* by Kord Davis with Doug Patterson (O'Reilly). Copyright 2012 Kord Davis, 978-1-449-31179-7."

If you feel your use of code examples falls outside fair use or the permission given above, feel free to contact us at *permissions@oreilly.com*.

Safari® Books Online

Safari Books Online (*www.safaribooksonline.com*) is an on-demand digital library that delivers expert content in both book and video form from the world's leading authors in technology and business.

Technology professionals, software developers, web designers, and business and creative professionals use Safari Books Online as their primary resource for research, problem solving, learning, and certification training.

Safari Books Online offers a range of product mixes and pricing programs for organizations, government agencies, and individuals. Subscribers have access to thousands of books, training videos, and prepublication manuscripts in one fully searchable database from publishers like O'Reilly Media, Prentice Hall Professional, Addison-Wesley Professional, Microsoft Press, Sams, Que, Peachpit Press, Focal Press, Cisco Press, John

Wiley & Sons, Syngress, Morgan Kaufmann, IBM Redbooks, Packt, Adobe Press, FT Press, Apress, Manning, New Riders, McGraw-Hill, Jones & Bartlett, Course Technology, and dozens more. For more information about Safari Books Online, please visit us online.

How to Contact Us

Please address comments and questions concerning this book to the publisher:

O'Reilly Media, Inc.
1005 Gravenstein Highway North
Sebastopol, CA 95472
800-998-9938 (in the United States or Canada)
707-829-0515 (international or local)
707-829-0104 (fax)

We have a web page for this book, where we list errata, examples, and any additional information. You can access this page at *http://oreil.ly/ethics-big-data*.

To comment or ask technical questions about this book, send email to *bookques tions@oreilly.com*.

For more information about our books, courses, conferences, and news, see our website at *http://www.oreilly.com*.

Find us on Facebook: *http://facebook.com/oreilly*

Follow us on Twitter: *http://twitter.com/oreillymedia*

Watch us on YouTube: *http://www.youtube.com/oreillymedia*

Acknowledgments

This book benefited from a large and wide variety of people, ideas, input, and efforts. I'd like to acknowledge several of them and apologize in advance to those I may have forgotten.

First, thanks to Brian Smith, Rob Wiley, and Tom Williams at Exact Target, a company who not only does a wonderful job of incorporating their values into their organizational culture, but are on the forefront of learning how to turn big data technologies into useful tools. In many ways, the experience of working with them forged the motivation for this book. Numerous conversations, interviews, dinners, and lunches yielded a great deal of great thinking and material, and I hope I've represented our discussions well.

Those discussions wouldn't have been possible if not for the projects that gave them a platform through working with XPLANE, The Visual Thinking Company. There are many great folks—and talents—at XPLANE but several individuals made direct contributions to the book including Matt Adams, Stephanie Gioia, Dave King, and James Macanufo.

Aside from those with whom I work closely, there were various subject matter experts, from a wide variety of industries and disciplines, who graciously gave of their time and expertise to help work through various concepts and their implications. These include: Andrew Davis, Nigel Ballard; Jason Bobe, Erin Conroy, Pete Forsyth, Ezra Gollogly, Dion Hinchliffe, Erik Huddleston, Bill Hoffman, Max Niederhofer, Martha Koenig, and Adam Riggs.

A special individual who provided a great deal of subject matter expertise is Doug Patterson. His academic background, training, and expertise were valuable and informed much of the philosophical thinking here. His experience teaching business ethics and facilitating classroom discussion on highly conceptual topics meant he could quickly identify key ethical issues. He was a great resource to turn to in those moments when I needed clarity on more nuanced aspects of issues that had become complex.

A dedicated, informed, and rigorous group of technical reviewers gave the work the thrashing it deserved and I hope that their comments and input are reflected fairly—I know they made the work stronger. So, a special thanks to Terence Craig, Bob Gourley, Mary E. Ludloff, James Macanufo, and Cathy O'Neill.

Last, and certainly not least, are many friends and members of my community. I want to thank them from the bottom of my heart for their encouragement, faith, discussions, patience, sustenance, interest, and ongoing belief in the value of this project: Laura Allen, Jake Baker, Tad Bamford, Cari Carter, Collin Connon, Tanya Frantzen, Patrick Foss, Vincent Grace, Drew Hansen, Erica Hassinger, Geoff Rogers, Jodi Sweetman, Carisa Sprecher, Khris Soden, Ben Thompson, Paul Wille, Rob Woolsey, and Morgan Wu.

Finally, a great deal of gratitude and an explicit Thank You to the many folks at O'Reilly who have been a part of this effort.

Especially my primary editor Courtney Nash who, when I told her I was planning to write a self-published white paper on big data ethics, immediately started investigating whether anyone had signed up to do that for O'Reilly and offered to bring a proposal to the editorial group. Special thanks for recognizing the value of the topic, being its champion, and working diligently to help make sure the project continued to unfold productively—all while making the work read better in the process.

That also couldn't have happened without interim editor (while Courtney was working on a side project of her own—which resulted in a beautiful baby girl), Julie Steele. Julie stepped in graciously, in the middle of a very busy and important time, and helped make sure I stayed between the rails as the work moved forward.

And lastly, of course, thanks to Tim O'Reilly for creating an organization that would even consider publishing work on such a topic and for his discussion and insights on technology, culture, and community.

I hope you all enjoy the book and find it useful.

CHAPTER 1

Big Data, Big Impact

*A people that values its privileges above its
principles soon loses both.*
—Dwight D. Eisenhower

*I had chosen to use my work as
a reflection of my values.*
—Sidney Poitier

Target knows. Apple Computer knows, too. So do LinkedIn, Netflix, Facebook, Twitter, Expedia, national and local political campaigns, and dozens of other organizations that all generate enormous economic, social, and political value. They know that that the age of Big Data is here and it's here to stay. The swelling ranks of organizations that increasingly depend on big-data technologies include dozens of familiar names and a growing number you've never heard of.

On February 16, 2012, the *New York Times* published an article about Target's ability to identify when a customer is pregnant. Target declined to comment or participate in the story, but it was written and published anyway. The onslaught of commentary and subsequent news raised numerous questions ranging from the legality of Target's actions to the broader public concern about private, personal information being made more public.

On April 20, 2011, two security researchers announced that iPhones were regularly recording the position of each device to a hidden file. While Apple readily acknowledged that the claim was true, the resulting hubbub made clear that it was the method by which that file was generated and stored that caused security concerns. The decision to use that technological method had clear and direct ethical consequences in the real world.

Who was involved in making that decision? A lone engineer in a back room making the technology perform in the way that made the most sense? Was there a broader business discussion of whether that function should be available at all? To what level of detail were the security and other risks discussed?

In August of 2011, Facebook faced criticism when it was thought to be exposing the names and phone numbers of everyone in the contacts on mobile devices that used the "Contacts" feature of the Facebook mobile application. It responded and clarified how the feature worked and provided people with a method to remove that information from their Facebook account. Why wasn't that clarification and method provided in conjunction with releasing the feature in the first place?

In 2011, when the CEO of GoDaddy published a tweet about killing elephants in Africa and publicly supported the controversial Stop Online Piracy Act (SOPA), the negative customer response resulted in the domain registrar reportedly losing tens of thousands of customers. The Kenneth Cole brand was damaged when they were perceived to be using the political uprising in Cairo in the spring of 2011 to promote their products. Apologies and a damaged brand reputation followed. In 2010, Wal-Mart was alleged to be using a fake online community to build support for new stores in areas where the idea was not popular. One of the public relations firms was allegedly responsible.

As you are likely considering how your organization would respond in similar situations, consider the fact that all these examples share one common factor: big-data technology. As these examples show, one impact of big data is that actions have far greater consequences, at a more accelerated pace, and direct repercussions for a company's brand quality, customer relationships, and revenue. As a result, big data is *forcing* new considerations about our values and behavioral actions—especially as it gives more people more ways to engage, communicate, and interact. One outcome of this growing presence of big-data technology is that business operations are changing and increasing the sheer amount of information they generate so fast that the big data phenomenon is starting to raise ethical questions.

As Brad Peters recently wrote in *Forbes*, it literally "changes the social contract" (*http://www.forbes.com/sites/bradpeters/2012/07/12/the-age-of-big-data/*). The nature of that change is complex. One primary motivation for this work is to address both individuals and organizations and suggest that more explicit and transparent discussion is needed —a discussion that inherently contains ethical components.

And although those ethical topics are centered on individual people, the implications span a variety of areas. In the same way that big data raises personal privacy concerns, it generates new questions about personal identity, notably who owns our personal data and how the increased presence and availability of more data influence our reputations.

For both individuals and organizations, four common elements define what can be considered a framework for big data ethics:

Identity
> What is the relationship between our offline identity and our online identity?

Privacy
> Who should control access to data?

Ownership
> Who owns data, can rights to it be transferred, and what are the obligations of people who generate and use that data?

Reputation
> How can we determine what data is trustworthy? Whether about ourselves, others, or anything else, big data exponentially increases the amount of information and ways we can interact with it. This phenomenon increases the complexity of managing how we are perceived and judged.

Both individuals and organizations have legitimate interests in understanding how data is being handled. Regardless of your role in an organization, or if you even work in technology, nearly everyone's life is touched by big-data technology today. Which means this framework has the potential to inform both the benefits big data provides and the potential risks from unintended consequences for a truly staggering number of people.

As an example, New York Judge Gary Brown recently found that an IP address is not sufficient evidence to identify copyright infringers (*http://torrentfreak.com/judge-an-ip-address-doesnt-identify-a-person-120503/*). Although this legal finding was focused on copyright issues, it could have far-reaching implications for questions about all four elements of big-data ethics. If a person is not an IP address (and who, really, ever thought they were identical?), then can any data generated via a specific IP address be legitimately associated with a single, unique individual?

Digital marketers have struggled with this for years. But the risk of unintended consequences as big data evolves becomes more widespread—well beyond targeted marketing. Consider how Google filters its understanding of your content preferences if you share equal time on the same computer with one or more people in your household. My interest in beach vacation spots is much less relevant to someone with whom I might share my Internet connection who is afraid of the ocean and can't swim. Improving the relevancy of targeted marketing is a major challenge, but the challenges and potential risks don't end with online advertising.

A realistic scenario illustrates some of the challenges people and organizations face. Imagine that an elderly relative's glucose and heart monitoring device shares the same IP address as the rest of your household. As a matter of course, all data from those medical devices is captured and stored by a healthcare provider. Now imagine that through an internal data leak, the hospital inadvertently mixes up their medical condition with your own. After all, you both live at the same address, could be the same gender, and might have the same last name.

This is not an economic risk, although it's easy to imagine bills for healthcare services being assigned to the wrong person as a result of the mix-up. But the legal decoupling of an IP address from a specific, individual person points to the presence of risks that exist right now, with technology that is already in widespread usage. The risk is that although there is value and benefit to healthcare innovations using technology, the real-world relationship between the Internet technologies used and the people who benefit from them is not sufficiently understood.

"Spoofing" (pretending to be someone you're not) has a long and storied history—both on and off the Internet. But in this scenario, the unintentional confusion between a relative's medical condition and your own, which is based on the assumption that a single person generates data originating via a single IP address, could have disastrous consequences if you're ever rushed to the emergency room.

Judge Brown's legal decision encourages a must-needed exploration of the nuances of privacy, identity, reputation, and data ownership. The direct impact of failing to understand the complexities and nuance of the relationships between big-data technologies and the people who use them can, in this example, literally be a matter of life and death.

Why Big Data?

At this point you might be asking, "Why not just *any* data?" After all, many organizations have been struggling to figure out how to manage their data for some time now, right? Common definitions of the popular phrase for the phenomenon "big data" are based on distinctions between the capabilities of legacy database technologies and new data storage and processing techniques and tools such as Hadoop clusters, Bloom filters, and R data analysis tools. Big data is data too big to be handled and analyzed by traditional database protocols such as SQL (which makes *big data* a term that may evolve over time; what is now big data may quite rapidly become small). In this sense, size is just one aspect of these new technologies. The risks and ethical considerations also come from a few related factors.

The *volume, variety,* and *velocity* of available information exponentially increase the complexity of information that companies need to manage, and these factors generate questions they haven't previously encountered in the course of doing business.

The volume at which new data is being generated is staggering. We live in an age when the amount of data we expect to be generated in the world is measured in exabytes and zettabytes. By 2025, the forecast is that the Internet will exceed the brain capacity of everyone living on the entire planet.

Additionally, the variety of sources and data types being generated expands as fast as new technology can be created. Performance metrics from in-car monitors, manufacturing floor yield measurements, all manner of healthcare devices, and the growing number of Smart Grid energy appliances all generate data.

More importantly, they generate data at a rapid pace. The velocity of data generation, acquisition, processing, and output increases exponentially as the number of sources and increasingly wider variety of formats grows over time. It is widely reported that some 90% of the world's data has been created in the last two years (*http://www.econo mist.com/node/21537967*). The big data revolution has driven massive changes in the ability to process complex events, capture online transactional data, develop products and services for mobile computing, and process many large data events in near real time.

In the last few years of working with organizations who use big data technologies, it became clear to us that there were divided opinions on just what were the ethical issues and constraints in a dizzying variety of big-data situations. Without a formal and explicit framework for having ethical discussions in business environments, people often revert to their own moral code. Which, although it's a great place to start, can quickly devolve into a "But, that's creepy..."/"No, it's not" debate that goes nowhere fast. What frequently happens in those cases is that the discussion becomes mired by frustration, the meeting ends, and the question doesn't get answered. The potential for harm due to unintended consequences can quickly outweigh the value the big-data innovation is intended to provide.

So, while business innovators are excited about the potential benefits they can create from the design and development of a wide range of new products and services based on big-data technologies, the size, variety, and velocity of information available raises new questions. Some of those questions are about the implications of the acquisition, storage, and use of large quantities of data about people's attributes, behavior, preferences, relationships, and locations.

Fundamentally, these questions are *ethical*. They relate to your values and how we apply them while creating products and services. And your values are at the heart of how you balance the promise of useful innovation against the risk of harm. Whether you are aware of them or not, your values inform how you conceive of and execute on designs for products and services based largely on information gleaned from massive amounts of data. They are critical inputs to the calculus you perform when weighing the promise of those benefits against the risks of unintended consequences.

This implies that there is a balance to be achieved between those risks and the benefits of the innovations that big data can provide. This book is intended, in part, to help organizations develop a framework for having explicit ethical discussions to help maintain that balance.

What Is Big Data Forcing?

Society, government, and the legal system have not yet adapted to the coming age of big-data impacts such as transparency, correlation, and aggregation. New legislation is being drafted, debated, and ratified by governments all over the world at a rapid pace.

Only a generation or two ago, one could fairly easily drop "off the grid" and disappear within the continental United States. Today, it would be nearly impossible for a person to do much of anything without generating a data trail that a reasonably knowledgeable and modestly equipped investigator could follow to its end (*http://www.wired.com/vanish/2009/11/ff_vanish2/*).

Big data is persistent. And it is persistent in a way that business and society have never experienced before. The Library of Congress is archiving all tweets since 2006. And when the Library of Congress archives something, they intend for it to *stay* archived. Facebook has tacitly acknowledged that deleting your account does not delete all the data associated with your account (*http://arstechnica.com/gadgets/2012/05/on-facebook-deleting-an-app-doesnt-delete-your-data-from-their-system/*).

Eric Freeman and David Gelernter coined the phrase "lifestream" to describe:[1]

> "…a time-ordered stream of documents that functions as a diary of your electronic life; every document you create and every document other people send you is stored in your lifestream. The tail of your stream contains documents from the past (starting with your electronic birth certificate). Moving away from the tail and toward the present, your stream contains more recent documents—papers in progress or new electronic mail; other documents (pictures, correspondence, bills, movies, voice mail, software) are stored in between. Moving beyond the present and into the future, the stream contains documents you will need: reminders, calendar items, to-do lists."

Freeman and Gelernter intended lifestream to inform software architectures and structures for managing personal electronic information, but the concept is useful in understanding how the persistence of big data influences critical, essential characteristics of individual lives. Big data often includes "metadata," which can add another layer (or several layers) of information about each of us as individuals onto the physical facts of our existence. For example, the architecture and technology of big data allows the location of where you physically were when you made a tweet to be associated with each message.

And those additional layers are explicit. They can contain a vast array of ancillary information only tangentially related to the essence of any given financial or social transaction. Big data can reconstruct your entire travel history anywhere on the planet. It supplies the information necessary to tie together intentionally disparate facets of your personality in ways we sometimes cannot fully control. Pictures of you on spring break are presumably not intended to be considered as relevant material when applying for a job, and big data has significantly changed how reputation is managed in such situations.

This data trail is just one example of how big-data technologies allow broader and deeper insight into human behavior and activity than ever before. Innovators of all types have

---

1. *http://cs-www.cs.yale.edu/homes/freeman/lifestreams.html*

realized the potential for turning those insights into new and valuable products and services. This wealth of data promises to improve marketing, management, education, research and development, healthcare, government, services, and a host of other aspects of our lives. Big data is already being used to improve insights into effective education policies and to improve our ability to predict dangerous weather conditions in microclimate-sized geographies.

But the forcing function big data creates raises questions about data handling with a new urgency. These challenges are potentially troubling because they often extend beyond the management controls of a single organization. Big-data technologies influence the very meaning of important concepts such as privacy, reputation, ownership, and identity for both individuals and corporations. As information is aggregated and correlated by not only the originating entity, but also by those who may seek to further innovate products and services using the original information, we frequently don't (or can't, even) control how that information is used once it is out of our hands.

Big data also allows us to congregate in online communities whose populations sometimes exceed those of entire countries. Facebook is the most well known example, but there are literally thousands of online communities across the Internet, each of which contains specific, unique snippets or facets of information about each of its members. We are just now realizing the impact of this phenomenon on our identities, the concept of ownership, how we view ourselves and our relationships, trust, reputation, and a host of other, more traditionally self-managed aspects of our lives.

Because the data is frequently data about people and their characteristics and behavior, the potential use and abuse of this acquired data extends in a great many directions. Direct benefits are now being realized, but concerns about the consequences of having personal data captured, aggregated, sold, mined, re-sold, and linked to other data (correlated) are just now beginning to see the light of day.

And these risks are not just limited to individual people. They apply equally, if not more, to organizations. Corporations are not in the business of harming their customers. Hospitals are not in the business of violating their patients' confidentiality. Nonprofit research facilities are not in the business of sharing their test subjects' personally identifiable information. Yet, through the normal course of everyday business operations, which increasingly utilize big-data technologies, the risk of various harms increases.

And the type, size, and impact of those risks are difficult to determine in advance. We have, as a society, only just begun to understand the implications of the age of big data.

Consider the following:

- The social and economic impact of setting insurance rates based on browser or location history, e.g., visits to sites with information about chest pain or a detailed record of your vehicle's GPS history (*http://www.wired.com/threatlevel/2011/09/onstar-tracks-you/*).

OnStar quickly reversed its decision in response to privacy concerns. See *http://www.computerworld.com/s/article/9220337/ OnStar_reverses_course_on_controversial_GPS_tracking_plans*.

- The use of genetic information to influence hiring practices.
- "Predicting" criminal behavior through extrapolation from location, social network, and browsing data. *Minority Report*–style "predictive policing" is already in place in some major urban areas (see *http://www.cbsnews.com/ 8301-18563_162-57412725/lapd-computer-program-prevents-crime-by-predicting-it/*).
- Retrieval of metadata about a person based on a picture snapped with a mobile phone in a "dating" app that gave access to criminal records, browsing history, or a site of dating reviews of individual people.

At risk are the very benefits of big data innovation itself. In late 2011 and early 2012, the Stop Online Piracy Act (SOPA) put before Congress was met with fierce resistance from a wide variety of industries, organizations, and individuals. The primary reason was the belief that the provisions of the proposed law would severely constrain innovation in the future using technical tools such as big data (*http://en.wikipedia.org/wiki/ Stop_Online_Piracy_Act*).

Part of the debate centered around the belief that the members of Congress supporting the bill were either misinformed by interested parties about how the technology worked and how innovation was made possible, or they were just simply unaware of the realities of how Internet and big data technologies worked in the first place. In either case, SOPA represents a classic example of how a lack of transparent and explicit discourse about how a critical piece of our economy and society works had the potential to significantly limit our collective ability to benefit from those tools.

As big data's forcing function drives data further into our organizations and individual lives, balancing risk and innovation will continue to be an urgent need that must be met in order to maintain the ability of big data to generate benefit rather than harm.

Big Data Is Ethically Neutral

While big-data technology offers the ability to connect information and innovate new products and services for both profit and the greater social good, it is, like all technology, ethically neutral. That means it does not come with a built-in perspective on what is right or wrong or what is good or bad in using it. Big-data technology has no value framework. Individuals and corporations, however, do have value systems, and it is only by asking and seeking answers to ethical questions that we can ensure big data is used in a way that aligns with those values.

Such discussions require explicitly exploring those values and developing ethical perspectives, which can be difficult. Ethics is a highly personal topic and comes loaded with lots of polarizing vocabulary, such as *good, bad, right,* and *wrong.* We all have personal moral codes, which naturally vary from individual to individual. The lack of a common vocabulary for expressing the relationship between what we personally believe in and what we, as members of a common enterprise, plan to do with big data can create constraints on productive discussion and obstacles to finding consensus.

That said, this isn't a book about dictating operational policies or changes to case or statute law. Business executives, managers, judges, and elected officials must see to that. This also isn't a book about business ethics—at least as traditionally conceived. Business is concerned primarily with profit and innovation. Ethical inquiries, as a formal practice, are of interest only as far as they impact profitable operations and the ongoing development of products and services that meet the needs of a dynamic market.

There is, however, an inherently social component to business, and in fact, big data and social media have only exaggerated this reality in recent years. The mere act of conducting commerce, exchanging goods and services for items of value (often in the form of currency), is an activity that typically involves people. And people have values. The purpose of this book is to build a framework for facilitating ethical discussions in business environments designed to expose those values and help organizations take actions that align with them.

The big-data forcing function is bringing business functions and individual values into greater contact with each other. Big data is pushing corporate action further and more fully into individual lives through the sheer volume, variety, and velocity of the data being generated. Big-data product design, development, sales, and management actions expand their influence and impact over individuals' lives in ways that may be changing the common meaning of words like *privacy, reputation, ownership,* and *identity.*

Its sheer size and omnipresence is essentially forcing new questions into play about our identities, the evolution of personal privacy, what it means to own data, and how our online data trails influence our reputations—both on- and offline. Organizations from business to education and from research to manufacturing and professional services have tremendous amounts of information available about their customers, their operations, and nearly every other measurable aspect of their existence. Before the rapid growth of big-data technology in the last five years, changes in organizational processes or policies had a delayed effect on customer's lives, if any. Whether a customer's personal data was accessible or not was typically a matter of how many individuals or organizations had access to customer records.

Big data operates at such a scale and pace now that such changes in policies and practices extend further and faster and touch more people. Thus, changes in business functions have a much greater impact on people's lives. The expansion of traditional operations touches our lives every day in ways we can hardly keep track of, let alone manage. The reality is that the ways in which legislation, social norms, economics, or reasonable expectations of normal interaction will change as a result of the growing presence of big data is simply unknown.

And it is precisely because these things are unknown that ethical dialog should be encouraged. Open and explicit dialog about aligning values with actions to balance the risks with the benefits of big-data innovations is one method you can use to ensure that you negotiate the trade-off well—and in your favor. Identifying those moments when decisions turn into actions, or *ethical decision points*, is the first step to developing a capacity to have those discussions both "in-the-room" on the fly and more formally in the development of transparent perspectives and policies.

Don't Tell Me What to Do

It is also not the aim of this book to be prescriptive, in the sense of laying down some hard-and-fast list of rules for the ethical handling of data. Indeed, these issues are often too specialized to a given business model, sector, or industry to allow for that. The aim, rather, is to illustrate the benefits of directly addressing these questions, to discuss key factors that go into developing a coherent and consistent approach for ethical inquiry, and to set out a framework for and encourage discussion. This discussion can take place not just in boardrooms, executive meetings, courtrooms, and legislatures, but also in working meetings, hallways, and lunchrooms—a discussion that is explicit, collaborative, and transparent.

The goal of addressing these questions directly through explicit and transparent dialog is to better understand and mitigate risks to relationships with customers and partners, and to better express the benefits of big-data innovations. Unfavorable perceptions and bad press affect the bottom line. Even the *perception* of unethical data handling creates a risk of negative consequences, diminishing internal support for business goals and external relationships with customers. This is not merely a question of transparency or good management; it is a broader ethical question about maintaining the consistent alignment of actions and values as big data evolves and becomes even more embedded and influential in people's lives.

In short, this book won't tell you what to do with your data. The intent is to help you engage in productive ethical discussions raised by today's big-data-driven enterprises, propose a framework for thinking and talking about these issues, and introduce a methodology for aligning actions with values within an organization. That framework will provide a set of tools that any enterprise can adopt to become an organization in which customers, partners, and other stakeholders can trust to act in accordance with explicit values coherently and consistently.

Important Concepts and Terms

Identifying ethical decision points helps to develop perspectives and policies that drive values alignment in business operations, products, and services involving personal data. To do that, you have to know what values you have and where they might not be aligned. And this can be a complex activity with a specialized vocabulary. The following are some useful terms in developing that vocabulary:

Rights and interests

It is common for people to speak of privacy *rights*, but talk of rights brings with it the suggestion that such rights are absolute, which presumes to prejudge some of the issues at hand. In order to avoid prejudgment, we will speak of privacy *interests* and other sorts of interests, with the explicit understanding that a right is a kind of interest, the strongest and most absolute kind.

For example, an absolute privacy right with respect to the usage of your medical data includes the right to stipulate that no privacy risk at all is to be taken with this data. But suppose that you are brought unconscious to the emergency room and treated—with data being generated in the process. This data might be useful in the development of better treatments for you and others in your situation. Do we really want to hold that the use or sharing of this data without your consent is absolutely forbidden? Even with the next nurse or doctor on staff? Perhaps we do want to hold that there is such a right, but to think that there is one should be an outcome, not a presupposition of the sort of discussion that we advocate.

This is all complicated by the fact that to have such a right is itself an ethical view. Supporting an absolute right inherently contains an ethical position and diminishes an ability to be objective about whether or not that position aligns with our values. Thinking in terms of privacy interests (as opposed to rights) allows for more objective freedom in assessing the strength of ethical claims.

Personal data

The commonly assumed distinction between *personally identifying information* and other data is largely an artifact of technological limitations that often can be overcome. In order to move forward, we need a very broad term for the sort of data that is at issue when people are concerned about privacy. In usage here, *personal data* will simply be any data generated in the course of a person's activities.

A responsible organization

The difference between doing right and doing what various people *think* is right is a significant one for the present topic. A *responsible organization* is an organization that is concerned both with handling data in a way that aligns with its values and with being perceived by others to handle data in such a manner. Balancing these two nonequivalent concerns is something a responsible organization must work to achieve.

So, big data is big, fast, and can contain a wide variety of information. It's here to stay, and it offers huge promise of economic gain, social benefit, and cultural evolution. And it's forcing ethical questions into places and environments where previously they haven't been critical to answer. How are people and organizations supposed to respond? This book advocates learning how to engage in explicit, transparent, and productive ethical inquiry.

The next chapters discuss how that kind of ethical inquiry can help align your values with your actions to both enhance innovation and to reduce risks. The discussion begins with a demonstration that ethical misalignment is present in even the most successful and well-run organizations, and then offers a vocabulary and a framework for engaging in the ethical inquiry needed to gain better alignment.

CHAPTER 2

Values and Actions

*People must have righteous principles
in the first, and then they will not fail
to perform virtuous actions.*

—Martin Luther

Asking ethical questions in business contexts can feel unusual at best and uncomfortable at worst. But as noted in the previous chapter, big data, like all technology, is ethically neutral. Technology does not come with a built-in perspective on what is right or wrong or good or bad when using it. Whereas big data is ethically neutral, the *use* of big data is not. Individuals and corporations are the only ones who can answer those questions, and so it's important to work past any discomfort.

And while big data represents both tremendous opportunity (in the form of new products and services) for broad business and social benefit, the opposite side of that coin is that it also represents serious risk. Finding and maintaining a balance between the benefits of innovation and the detriments of risks is, in part, a function of ethical inquiry.

Developing a capability to find and maintain that balance is partially ethical because of the essential nature of the technology itself. Digital business transactions (such as buying things online) and digital social interactions (such as sharing photos on social networks) inherently capture information related to, but distinct from, the data itself.

For example, showing your nephew's picture to a friend at a holiday party leaves a faint, shallow record of that event that exists only in your memory and the memory of the person you shared it with. Posting your nephew's photo on a social network not only creates a nearly permanent record of that sharing action, but also includes a surprisingly wide variety of information that is ancillary to the actual sharing itself. To the degree that there is a record of the simple act of sharing photos online, it contains a great deal of information.

Ethics come into play, in part, when organizations realize that information has value that can be extracted and turned into new products and services. The degree to which ethics play a role in this process is, of course, more complicated than a simple identification of which information is "ancillary" and which is not. The ethical impact is highly context-dependent. But to ignore that there *is* an ethical impact is to court an imbalance between the benefits of innovation and the detriments of risk.

Articulating Your Values

Organizations that fail to explicitly and transparently evaluate the ethical impacts of the data they collect from their customers risk diminishing the quality of their relationships with those customers, exposing their business to the risks of unintended consequences. Ethical evaluation includes both an understanding of how an organization will utilize the customer data that describes an enormously wide variety of historical actions, characteristics, and behaviors (data-handling practices) and an understanding of the values that organization holds.

Many values are already implicit in business decisions. Companies value happy clients and elegant product designs; employees value productive working environments and fair compensation packages. People and companies value collaboration and innovation. Some of these values are derived from the many business drivers for "doing the right thing." Additionally, specific legal or policy requirements exist in many industries. Entire business functions are devoted to aligning those values with the business decisions and the subsequent actions we take every day.

Fortunately, you already know how to ensure that your values are being honored in the course of conducting business operations. You do it all the time. In many product design (and other) endeavors, there often comes a moment when the question is asked, "Are we doing the right thing?" or "Is this the right solution?"

In this context, the word *right* can mean many things. It can mean: Are we meeting the customer's expectations? Is the design solution appropriate to the problem? Are we honoring the scope of the work? Is this a profitable feature to add to our product? Will people buy this? It can also mean: Do we agree that this action is acceptable to perform based on our values?

But when you ask, "Are we doing the right thing?" in the ethical sense, the place to start is not with a discussion of identity, privacy, reputation, or ownership (or any of a number of other important topics). Big-data ethics are not about one particular issue. Individual, specific concerns (including, of course, privacy) are absolutely important. But they are important as expressions of actions you take in accordance with your values. Ethical practices are an *outcome* of ethical inquiry. And while a coherent and consistent privacy policy is one possible outcome of ethical inquiry, it is far from the only possible outcome.

For example, Google's decision not to allow pseudonyms on their Google+ social network is partially the result of an ethical inquiry into what constitutes a person's identity. A different kind of value judgment is made when a company debates whether it is acceptable (the "right thing") to sell anonymized data to third-party entities. Consumer protection laws such as HIPAA reflect the outcome of ethical discussions about the government's obligations to shield individuals from the unauthorized sharing of personal medical histories. And copyright and trademark infringement concepts are derived from answering questions about who rightly owns what, for how long, and what use others can make of the created material—that is, what we value about the creation of new works and how we define the domain of ownership.

Values are also the place to start an ethical inquiry when designing products and services using big-data technologies. It would be a surprise if any organization explicitly stated that they did not value individual identity in some fashion. But, for instance, the question is not, "How should we, as a corporation, define an individual's identity?" The ethical question is more centrally interested in what the company should value regarding specific aspects of a person's identity, and how they should value it in the company's individual and organizational actions.

One benefit of starting with value principles is a firmer foundation for subsequent action and decision-making. That foundation can also serve to drive increased efficiency and innovation across the board.

Teams, departments, and organizations of all types operate more effectively when they share a common set of values. Roy Disney, nephew of Walt Disney and founder of a business well known for driving creativity and innovation to enormous business and social benefit, said, "It's not hard to make decisions when you know what your values are." Instead of teams wasting time asking, "Should we be doing this," a sense of *explicitly* shared values removes barriers and constraints to productivity and creative problem solving, turning the question into, "How *can* we do this?"

Turning Values into Actions

Focused action does not directly follow from shared values. A productive dialog about the appropriate action to take in support of shared values is dependent on an understanding of what those values and possible actions are.

Many people are already beginning to have this dialog. A broad range of organizations and institutions are working to align their values and actions. And ethical questions are being asked about big data in working meetings, at dinner parties, in industry groups, in legislatures across the world, and even in the US Supreme Court.

For instance, the World Economic Forum recently launched a multiyear project called "Rethinking Personal Data," which is exploring opportunities for economic growth and social benefit in light of barriers that restrict personal data movement and protection.

As part of that initiative, the Forum defined personal data as a "new economic asset," thus opening wide opportunities for data market innovations—not to mention a range of unanswered questions about who owns what (*http://www.weforum.org/issues/ rethinking-personal-data*).

These represent broad-based concern and inquiry into whether or not big data is honoring our values. But we simply must get better at having collective, productive discussions about how ethics inform our values and actions. Big data is already outpacing our ability to understand its implications. Businesses are innovating every day, and the pace of big-data growth is practically immeasurable.

To provide a framework for dissecting the often nuanced and interrelated aspects of big data ethics, the following key components can help untangle the situation.

Four Elements of Big-Data Ethics: Identity, Privacy, Ownership, and Reputation

Identity

Inquiries about identity are related in similar ways. Christopher Poole, creator of 4chan, gave a compelling talk at Web 2.0 in 2011, introducing the idea that identity is "prismatic" (*http://www.wired.com/business/2011/10/you-are-not-your-name-and-photo-a-call-to- re-imagine-identity/*). He emphasized that who we are—our identity—is multifaceted and is hardly ever summarized or aggregated in whole for consumption by a single person or organization. The implication is that if our identity is multifaceted, then it's likely that our values and ethical relationship to identity are also multifaceted.

Expressing a seemingly opposing view, Mark Zuckerberg recently made the assertion that having more than one identity demonstrates a "lack of integrity" (*http:// www.nytimes.com/2011/05/14/technology/14facebook.html*).

If our historical understanding of what identity means is being transformed by big-data technologies (by providing others an ability to summarize or aggregate various facets of our identity), then understanding our values around the concept itself enhances and expands our ability to determine appropriate and inappropriate action. Big data provides others the ability to quite easily summarize, aggregate, or correlate various aspects of our identity—without our participation or agreement.

If big data is evolving the meaning of the concept of identity itself, then big data is also evolving our ethical relationship to the concept the word represents. Which makes it easy to understand the value of explicit dialog and inquiry. The more our actions are fully aligned with the evolution and expansion of identity, the more fully and explicitly we can understand the values motivating them.

Privacy

If it is true that big data (and technology in general) is changing the meaning of the word "privacy," then we all benefit by exploring what those changes are through a discussion of what is valuable *about* privacy. Understanding what is valuable about various aspects of privacy, even in light of recent rapid transformations, is helpful when deciding what action we should and should not take to honor individual privacy.

Plenty of people would argue that we have gained a degree of control over how the world perceives us. Political dissidents in Egypt can express their views online in a way that no other medium, technology, or context allows them to speak—or be heard. Victims of abuse or people who suffer from the same disease can share their experiences and gain an invaluable sense of connection and community through the use of ostensibly anonymous online identities.

These perspectives, however, motivate the question: have we lost or gained control over our ability to manage how the world perceives us?

In 1993, the *New Yorker* famously published a cartoon with canines at the keyboard whose caption read: "On the Internet, nobody knows you're a dog" (*http://en.wikipe dia.org/wiki/On_the_Internet,_nobody_knows_you%27re_a_dog*). At the time, this was funny because it was true. Today, however, in the age of prevalent big data, it is not only possible for people to know that you're a dog, but also what breed you are, your favorite snacks, your lineage, and whether you've ever won any awards at a dog show.

In those instances where an individual intentionally keeps any information about their identity private, at least one ethical question arises: what right do others have to make it public? If there are personal interests that naturally arise as a matter of creating that information, is the mere act of transferring it to a database (or transmitting it via the Internet) sufficient to transfer the rights associated with its creation? Extensive rights are granted to the creators of artistic works. Can the creation of data about ourselves be considered a creative act? Does our mere existence constitute a creative act? If so, then do not all the legal protections associated with copyright law naturally follow?

Further, is each facet of one's identity subject to the same private/public calculus? By what justification can one organization correlate information about a person's health history with information about their online searches and still claim to be honoring all facets equally? A common assumption is that these offline expectations ought to be reflected in our ability to manage that behavior online and maintain an (at least functionally) equal set of expectations. A critical topic in the privacy element of big data is the question: is that assumption true?

There are two issues. First, does privacy mean the same thing in both online and offline in the real world? Second, should individuals have a legitimate ability to control data about themselves, and to what degree?

Frequently, these discussions boil down to distinctions between offline behavior and online expectations. In the same way that we can ask of others what justification allows them to turn private-by-choice information into public data, we can ask of ourselves: why do we expect the ability to self-select and control which facets we share with the world online to be the same as it is offline?

The difference between online and offline expectations regarding the degree of control individuals have over open access to data about themselves is a deeply ethical inquiry. What value do people place on benefiting from a loss of control of their data (letting others use it in novel, innovative, and beneficial ways) versus the risk of that data being used in ways that may harm them? It was funny that 20 years ago on the Internet no one would know you're a dog because technology allowed us to extend the ability to maintain anonymity to its extreme. Indeed, for many years, one could operate in almost complete anonymity on the Internet. And many did. To what degree has big data removed that ability from our individual choice and placed it in the hands of others?

The goal is to understand how to balance the benefits of big-data innovations with the risks inherent in sharing more information more widely.

Reputation

As recently as that *New Yorker* cartoon (19 years ago), reputation consisted primarily of what people—specifically those who knew and frequently interacted with you—knew and thought about you. Unless we were famous for some other reason, the vast majority of us managed our reputation by acting well (or poorly) in relation to those directly around us. In some cases, a second-degree perception—that is, what the people who knew you said about you to the people who they knew—might influence one's reputation.

Before this gets all recursive, remember that the key characteristic is how reputation has changed. One of the biggest changes born from big data is that now the number of people who can form an opinion about what kind of person you are is exponentially larger and farther removed than it was even a few short years ago. And further, your ability to manage or maintain your online reputation is growing farther and farther out of individual control. There are entire companies now whose entire business model is centered on "reputation management" (see *http://en.wikipedia.org/wiki/Reputation_management*).

We simply don't know how our historical understanding of how to manage our reputation translates to digital behavior. At a minimum, this is sufficient reason alone to suggest further inquiry.

Ownership

Along similar lines, the degree of ownership we hold over specific information about us varies as widely as the distinction between privacy rights and privacy interests. Do we, in the offline world, "own" the facts about our height and weight? Does our existence itself constitute a creative act, over which we have copyright or other rights associated with creation? Does the information about our family history, genetic makeup, and physical description, preference for Coke or Pepsi, or ability to shoot free throws on the basketball court constitute property that we own? Is there any distinction between the ownership qualities of that information? If it does, then how do those offline rights and privileges, sanctified by everything from the Constitution to local, state, and Federal statues, apply to the online presence of that same information?

 In February 2012, The White House unveiled a blueprint for a consumer "Bill of Rights" intended to enhance protections for individual privacy and how personal information is used online. See *http://www.white house.gov/the-press-office/2012/02/23/we-can-t-wait-obama-administration-unveils-blueprint-privacy-bill-rights*.

In fact, there are more than a dozen initiatives and programs designed to create a codified set of principles or guidelines to inform a broad range of ethical behavior online.

As open data markets grow in size and complexity, open government data becomes increasingly abundant, and companies generate more revenue from the use of personal data, the question of who owns what—and at what point in the data trail—will become a more vocal debate.

Benefits of Ethical Inquiry

These short discussions illustrate what an ethical inquiry can look like. Ethical inquiry originating from an exploration of values exposes ethical questions in a way that allows them to be answered in more useful fashions. And while aligning business values with customer values has obvious benefits, big data creates a broader set of ethical concerns. Merely echoing the currently prevailing public opinion is shortsighted at best; there are other significant benefits available through aligning values and actions as an outcome of explicit ethical inquiry. Organizations fluent in big-data ethics can contribute much to broader discussions of how they are impacting people's lives. The strategic value of taking a leadership role in driving the alignment of ethical values and action has benefits both internally and externally.

Those benefits can include:

- Faster consumer adoption by reducing fear of the unknown (how are you using my data?)
- Reduction of friction from legislation from a more thorough understanding of constrains and requirements
- Increased pace of innovation and collaboration derived from a sense of purpose generated by explicitly shared values
- Reduction in risk of unintended consequences from an overt consideration of long-term, far-reaching implications of the use of big-data technologies
- Social good generated from leading by example

These benefits are achieved, in part, through an intentional set of alignment actions. And those are necessarily informed by an understanding of what shared values members of a common enterprise hold. Discovering those values through explicit inquiry and developing a common vision of the actions an organization takes in support of those values influences how you conceive of and treat individual identity, personal privacy, and data ownership, and how you understand potential impacts on customer's reputations in the design, development, and management of products and services.

In reality, these ethical discussions can be avoided completely. It's easy—just don't have them. After all, it's easier to ask for forgiveness than permission, right? And if you don't ask the questions, you're not responsible for not having the answers. But policy decisions are made, technical innovations are designed, and new product features are rolled out, resulting in ethical implications, regardless of whether they're considered—ignoring them doesn't make them disappear. Avoiding those discussions only means that decisions get made without consideration for their ethical consequences, and in a way that may not accord with your values. Unfortunately, such a lack of attention to the ethical aspects of decision-making about data-handling practices is common.

Currently only two of the Fortune 50 corporations make any explicit, public policy statement citing any reason for the existence of their privacy policy other than, "You care about privacy, so we do, too." Which implies that, although most companies understand that people care about their privacy, they don't have a clear statement of which values their privacy policies support or why they support them.

Although it's entirely possible that any given policy actually does align with an organization's values, there is no way to know. The resulting confusion generates uncertainty and concern, both of which undermine long-lasting and trusting relationships.

What Do Values Have to Do with Anything?

Values inform the foundation for a framework of ethical decision-making simply because they are *what we believe in*. And we believe in all sorts of things. Truth, justice, the American way, Mom, apple pie, and Chevrolet are all familiar examples.

Historically, business has been more about the development of strategic plans for action and optimizing the execution of those plans to create profit. The forcing function of big data is expanding the ethical impact of our business operations further into the personal lives of its employees and customers. It is a direct result of the sheer volume, velocity, and variety of information big data allows businesses to utilize. Businesses used to make do with relatively shallow amounts of historical buying behavior, often limited to broad categories of information, such as how many of what products were purchased at a particular location during a specific timeframe. They could answer questions like "what color car is purchased most often in Texas in the summer?" or "this coffee shop on that street corner sells more than other locations."

Now a business can answer detailed questions like "how much toothpaste did your family buy from us in 2010—and what brands, at what frequency, and at exactly which time and place?" Reward cards associated with all kinds of goods and services know the detailed history of your purchases. That information can generate both savings benefits and annoying junk mail. Marketers of many flavors want very much to correlate that information with their products and services in hopes that they can target more compelling marketing messages. They want to turn information about your behaviors and actions in the world into knowledge about how to better influence your future decisions —and, thus, how to better inform their business strategies.

This is pure business gold. It is valuable across many business functions, ranging from designing new products and services (learning no one likes pineapple-flavored toothpaste) to building better supply chain and manufacturing models and processes to reduce costs (zip-code-level forecasting capabilities), and opening up whole new entire markets (on-demand discount offerings for last-minute hotel property cancellations).

It is increasingly difficult to "opt out" of the expansion of business operations into our lives. One can choose not to subscribe to a grocery store reward program—and accept the loss of the discounts those programs can provide. Although there is no requirement to join a social network, there can be a stigma attached to not doing so.

In 1987, Robert Bork's nomination to the Supreme Court was hotly contested, in part by using his video rental history as evidence in support of arguments against his confirmation. His reputation as a qualified candidate for the Supreme Court was being assessed, in part, by making judgments about the movies he watched. The resulting controversy led to Federal legislation enacted by Congress in 1988. Called the Video Privacy Protection Act, the VPPA made it illegal for any videotape service provider to disclose rental history information outside the ordinary course of business and made violators liable for damages up to $2,500.

In September 2011, Netflix posted a public appeal to customers to contact their Congressional representatives to amend the VPPA to allow for Netflix users to share their viewing history with friends on Facebook (*http://blog.netflix.com/2011/09/help-us-bring-facebook-sharing-to.html*). It was a mere 23 years between the passing of the VPPA, where Congress took action to protect consumers from having their purchase history used to judge their professional capabilities, and a major American business asking for customer support to allow that very same information to be shared legally.

Without big data, no business would even be in a position to offer such a capability or make such a request, and the question of whether we should change the law would be moot. And this is just one small example: the big-data forcing function extends business operations into the nooks and crannies of our lives in ways we have yet to discover.

In the 23 years between the VPPA and the Netflix request, big data has influenced our *actual values* and what we think is important, or not, to be able to share—and via which mechanisms and for what purposes. And it is precisely the force of that extension into our daily lives and the influence that it has on our actual values that motivates a call for more explicit discussion about the ethical use of big-data technologies.

At those moments when we do uncover another expansion of the influence of big data on our lives, ethical decision points help provide a framework for getting a handle on what we value and which actions are acceptable to us—all of which helps to create a balance between the benefits of innovation and the risk of harm.

Ethical Decision Points

Ethical decision points provide a framework for exploring the relationship between what values you hold as individuals—and as members of a common enterprise—and aligning those values with the actions you take in building and managing products and services utilizing big data technologies. We'll briefly introduce the vocabulary of ethical decision points here and describe in more detail how they can work in your organization in Chapter 4.

Ethical decision points consist of a series of four activities that form a continuous loop: Inquiry, Analysis, Articulation, and Action.

Inquiry: discovery and discussion of core organizational values

An understanding of what our values *actually* are (not what we *think* they are, or more removed, what we think *others* think they are)

Example: We value transparency in our use of big data.

Analysis: review of current, actual data-handling practices and an assessment of how well they align with core organizational values

The exploration of whether a particular use of big data technology aligns with the values that have been identified

Example: Should we build this new product feature using big data?

Articulation: explicit, written expression of alignment and gaps between values and practices

Clear, simple expressions of where values and actions align—and where they don't —using a common vocabulary for discussing whether proposed actions align with identified values

Example: This new product feature that uses big-data technology supports our value of transparency.

Action: tactical plans to close alignment gaps that have been identified and to encourage and educate on how to maintain that alignment as conditions change over time

Example: If we build this new product feature, we must explicitly share (be transparent) with our customers and ourselves how that feature will use personal data.

Ethical decision points generate a new type of organizational capability: the ability to conduct an ethical inquiry and facilitate ethical dialog. Such inquiry and discussion is frequently difficult, not only because it comes loaded with people's own personal value systems but also because business historically has not been focused on developing organizational capabilities to facilitate such activities. Big data is bringing values and ethics into product and service design processes, and this impacts a wide variety of operational capabilities that business historically has not developed a mature capacity to manage.

These ethical decision points can be identified by several methods. One familiar, if not entirely reliable or satisfactory, method is the "creepy" factor. This consists essentially of a visceral, almost automatic and involuntary feeling that *something isn't quite right*. It is often accompanied by an uncomfortable shifting in your chair or that slight tingling on the back of your neck. It's one of the feelings you can get when what you're experiencing is out of alignment with your expectations. Millions of people recently had that feeling when they realized that Target could tell when someone was pregnant merely based on buying behavior (*http://www.nytimes.com/2012/02/19/magazine/shopping-habits.html?pagewanted=all*).

"Creepy" is a useful but slippery concept. And the challenge to calculating the Creepy Quotient of value-to-action alignment in the context of your business model and operations is highly context-dependent. Exactly how dependent on context varies by factors too numerous to identify completely here, but general examples include variations in industry regulations, technology stack, or platform; existing or planned business partnerships; and intended usage. Healthcare has different regulatory requirements than retail sales. Some social networks provide built-in tools to rank a person's "reputation," but you don't expect financial management software to share your credit rating (one aspect of your financial reputation) with other individuals or organizations without your explicit permission.

So, although it's a familiar feeling and "creepy" can help us identify when we're facing an ethical decision point, it isn't quite robust enough to help guide us into a more comfortable ethical space. Questions follow immediately about what *kind* of creepy we're concerned about and exactly what to do (what action to take) about that feeling.

More helpful is to develop new methods and capabilities to explore the intuitions that form the basis of a visceral creepy response. There are natural avenues of inquiry into the precise nature of what can make us feel uncomfortable with certain aspects of big data. Motivated by individual moral codes, we can explore those values explicitly and uncover ways to bridge the gap between individual moral codes informed by our intuition and how we agree to proceed as members of a common enterprise. Encouraging the development of these methods is the broadest goal of this book.

One additional consideration is how to parse "creepy" into more useful terms. Big data itself creates an expanding series of "concentric circles of influence." The complex interactions and connections of big data create an ecosystem of ethics, at any given point of which there is a unique set of circumstances that influences how values show up and the implications of various actions taken using that data.

In this ecosystem, as particular pieces of data are used, reused, combined, correlated, and processed at each point of expansion, the impact of value alignment factors can vary considerably—and thus the creepy factor evolves the farther away you get from the point of origin. On the first use of a particular piece of data, creepy may be different than it is three or four steps down the road. What might be creepy if you do it today may be more or less creepy if you, or someone else farther down the data trail, do it three days from now. The fact that an online retailer knows that you buy a lot of outdoor equipment is less creepy when that same retailer uses that information to provide you with discounted merchandise offers than it would be if an unaffiliated third party sends an unsolicited offer for discounted spare parts to the exact model of camp stove you bought last year. Conversely, it might seem less creepy if an unaffiliated national environmental organization makes unsolicited contact to request a donation—especially if you share the same values.

Not to mention that negotiating the use of customer data with business partners brings an entirely new set of values into consideration. If it is complex to align your own organization's values and action, business partnerships increase the complexity with each touch point between your organization's use of customer data and theirs.

Other topics and vocabulary that often arise during ethical decision points include:

Intention

> The intentions of those who through direct or surreptitious means have access to the data in question

Security

> The security of this data in the hands of each entity in the data chain

Likelihood

> The probability that access to specific data would result in either benefit or harm

Aggregation

> The mixture of possibilities derived from correlating available data

Responsibility

> The various degrees of obligation that arise at each point in the data chain

Identity

> The single or multiple facets of characteristic description(s) that allow an individual to be uniquely individuated

Ownership

> The status of who holds what usage rights at each point in the data chain

Reputation

> The judgment(s) that may be derived from available data

Benefit

> The specific contribution or value available data is expected to make

Harm

> The sort of harm that might come from access to specific data

What Does All That Really Mean?

There are such things as values. We use and refer to them all the time. We even use them to make decisions about what actions we should or should not take in a wide variety of situations. We discuss them everywhere and often, and they form a critical part of the foundations for our laws, expected norms of social behavior, political action, financial behavior, and individual and group responsibility, and they, we hope, inform our vision of the future.

Big-data technology is expanding the sphere of where we need to apply value thinking. Not because big-data technology is inherently dangerous or because it is poorly understood, but because the volume, variety, and velocity of the data it produces and provides has reached the point where it has seeped into our daily lives in ways we have never seen before.

It touches those social, political, financial, and behavioral aspects of our lives with new considerations for the very way in which we understand and agree about the meaning of important words like identity, privacy, ownership, and reputation. The goal is not to understand how to amend those words to incorporate the changes big data brings. The goal also is not to change big data to incorporate our historical understanding of those words.

The goal is to develop a capacity to incorporate ethical inquiry into our normal course of doing business. An inquiry that is a way of talking about our values in the context of the actions we take in relationship to the opportunities that big data provides.

Learning to recognize and actively engage ethical decision points is one way to start building that capability. The basic framework helps us identify what our values actually are, understand whether they align with how we're using (or intend to use) big data, and develop a common vocabulary to discuss how best to achieve and support that alignment.

There are significant benefits to being able to talk about values in the usage of big data. A sense of shared values in an organization reduces barriers to productivity and innovation. Rather than debating whether we should do something (i.e., whether we collectively value the objective), we get right to taking action to achieve the objective (i.e., collectively working to reach the goal).

Consider any social, political, or religious organization. The Audubon Society and the National Rifle Association have very different goals, and their organizational values could hardly be more different.

But there is one characteristic that they, and many other organizations, share: their respective members share a common set of values. There may be disagreement among the ranks on occasion, and those values may shift and evolve over time, but it is clear that each organization spends a great deal of time explicitly engaged in discovering, articulating, and taking action based on their respective set of common values.

At least one of the many reasons for this engagement is that those organizations know that being clear and explicit about a shared set of common values increases their operational effectiveness. And, in the same way, as you learn how to maximize operations using big data, aligning your values with your actions also decreases the risk of unintended consequences. It won't eliminate those risks, of course, but an explicit ethical inquiry sustains a legitimate methodology for mitigating them—and often can provide organizations with a clear place to start when a response is required.

Let's explore now how values are currently being represented in the course of doing business today.

CHAPTER 3

Current Practices

I have always thought the actions of men the best interpreters of their thoughts.

—John Locke

Data can be useful or anonymous, but never both.

—Paul Ohm "Broken Promises of Privacy:
Responding to the Surprising Failure of
Anonymization," UCLA Law Review 57, p. 1702

If ethical practices are the result of ethical inquiry, then how do those practices show up in business today?

This chapter explores findings from primary and secondary research, including direct one-on-one interviews with industry thought leaders and practitioners working at companies who use big data.

Reading the privacy policies and other statements available on the websites of most organizations is a great way to understand how data-handling practices are showing up in the world today: they're free, available to anyone on the Web, and, although often written in fairly legal language, generally state in somewhat accessible terms what policies an organization follows when handling data.

We reviewed the public-facing policy statements of the top 50 Fortune 500 corporations to better understand the current state of affairs of data-handling practices and how they relate to users, consumers, and others.[1] The process included identifying specific policy elements across a number of data handling practices.

---

1. As of Fall 2011

Examples include:

- Whether data would be sold without consent
- If target advertising was utilized
- How much control customers had over the usage of their data
- Whether data would be purchased from other organizations
- If data was shared or aggregated
- Stated reasons for the policy itself

Taken together, the findings paint a picture of common practice in large enterprise environments. The broader implications, however, reveal issues with coherence and consistency in data-handling practices.

It is not surprising that different organizations have different practices—after all, different organizations have different values. What is somewhat surprising is the degree of differences across practices. There were clear trends and commonalities in many aspects, but the variations in how specific practices were carried out seem to indicate either that there is an amazingly wide variety of values driving corporate action or that organizations are just not sure exactly what they value (and, hence, what actions they should take to honor those values) in the first place.

Let's take a look at the findings first.

Findings Summary

- Of the 50 policies surveyed, 40 indicated that the corporation would share personal data with third-party service providers, such as suppliers and shippers.
- Of the remaining 10, 8 policies said nothing, and 2 stated that the corporation would not share personal information, even with third-party service providers.
- Of the 50 policies, 34 explicitly stated that the corporation would not sell personal data without consent.
  - No policy explicitly stated that the corporation would sell personal data.
- Of the 50 policies, 11 stated that the corporation would buy or otherwise "obtain" personal information from third parties.
  - No policy stated that a corporation would not buy personal information.
- Of the 50 policies, 23 stated that the corporation did engage in targeted advertising on third-party websites and through third-party marketing networks. Of the remainder, only one policy ruled out targeted advertising, while 26 said nothing about the topic.

- Of the 50 policies, 33 stated that a user could control the use of her data with respect to things like targeted advertising. Of these 33 policies, 31 explained how to opt out.

  — Of these 31 policies, 14 directed the user to a relatively convenient, web-based location for opting out. Of the 14 corporations offering a web-based opt-out, 5 employed the services of the Network Advertising Initiative.[2] Three of the remaining nine required the user to create an account on the site in order to opt out.

  — Of the 17 policies that offered an opt-out from targeted marketing that wasn't web-based, 14 gave an email address for the purpose. None of these made clear that the email in question would trigger an automatic opt-out. Other policies directed the reader to a phone number.

Buying Versus Selling

Consider the unequal treatment given to selling personal data versus buying it:

- 34 out of 50 Fortune-class companies said that they would *not sell* personal data.
- No company said explicitly that they *would sell* personal data.
- No company made any explicit statement that they would *not buy* personal data.
- 11 policies made explicit statements that buying personal data *was allowed*.

Without knowing any other facts, this seems strange: if it is not OK to sell something, how could it be OK to buy it?

If selling personal data is wrong because it may harm a third party (making the individual more susceptible to harm through unintended consequences), then it would seem to follow that buying personal data contributes as much as selling personal data does to the risk of harm through unintended consequences.

It's notoriously complicated to determine who is more responsible in exchanges that inherently contain risk, the "buyer" or the "seller." The judicial system frequently punishes sellers more than buyers. Since the buying and selling of personal data is (currently) legal, the question becomes even more nuanced. And there is active debate and frequent new legislation regarding consumer rights online all the time.

---

2. *http://www.networkadvertising.org/managing/opt_out.asp*

When an additional party gains access to personal data, there is almost certainly an increased risk of harm. The potential for weaker security and protection measures, differences in data-handling policy and practice, or the mere lack of insight into another organization's data-handling processes can contribute to the risk. Which raises the question of whether acquiring personal data (buying it) contributes as much to the degree of risk as selling it does.

There is, at least, one clear take-away: buying personal data is a common practice in current business models, but none of the Fortune 50 are comfortable enough with the practice to state publicly that they'll also sell it. This seems to indicate that organizations are more comfortable with some values than others—a value in itself that is showing up in their actions.

All of this buying and selling relates directly to one of the central topics in the debate over big-data handling today: targeted advertising. Though many people are concerned about having their viewing history follow them around the Internet, there are realistic scenarios that provide direct consumer benefit. It makes sense that since users are going to see advertising in any case, they might as well see ads for things in which they're more likely to be interested and it makes sense that tracking browsing behavior to infer what people are interested in is perfectly acceptable. For example, a recent browsing session exploring vacation activities in Bermuda can easily serve up targeted advertising on a national news site offering discounted hotel rates—and who doesn't want to save money on vacation?

The question here is: whose interests are being best served and are those the right priorities? In the absence of more information, any firm conclusions would be speculative. But even in the absence of explicit policy statements about selling personal data, it seems clear that *somebody* is selling it because a lot of organizations are buying it.

Opt-in Versus Opt-out

The opt-out model of providing customers control over the use of their data is the norm. In that model, the default configuration is to require people to take additional action ("opt-out") to prevent having their data used for other purposes. Frequently, the mere agreement to Terms of Services (whether you've read them or not) or the act of using a particular product online automatically grants permission to acquire personal data for use, for example, in targeted advertising. Although 33 out of 50 organizations offered people a way to control the use of their data, there is less uniformity in the *ease* of the opt-out procedure itself.

It is tempting to sympathize with this practice. It is difficult enough to get people to opt-in—even in the face of clear consumer benefits. We're all familiar with the feeling of risk from not really knowing how a company is going to use our personal information. Not to mention email boxes clogged full of useless or irrelevant offers. That's why many people create dummy email addresses when they sign up for some things and use other tricks to protect their privacy.

But even though it is simple and easy to fix that gap in customer's understanding, that fear of the unknown risk creates a barrier to conversion that all organizations are familiar with. Making it too easy to opt out can easily be seen as detrimental to both the consumer and the business model.

Even understanding the temptation to choose the path of least resistance in order to support specific business models, designing and implementing business processes and tools to make it less likely or more difficult for people to opt out begs the question of what values are motivating the choice of which model to implement. Which value is most important: acknowledging and respecting people's fear of the unknown risk and honoring their interest in reducing it, or making it slightly more difficult to support a business model?

These value questions become increasingly important as the evolution of big data unfolds. This is because as more data becomes available and easily analyzed on commodity hardware, the easier it will be to combine *initially* anonymous data sets with other data sets and correlate them to reveal new patterns or information. Some of which could cause unintended consequences, such as revealing damaging personal information.

Correlation Through Aggregation

Inconsistent policy statements on buying versus selling data and variations in opt-out procedures for uses such as targeted advertising indicate the need for deeper inquiry. The incoherence actually generates more distrust and confusion. Reducing the risk of the unknown, or not understanding what will happen to personal data, represents a substantial opportunity for organizations to share their values more broadly and align their actions with them more fully.

These can be complicated goals to achieve. Consider the aspects of the reviewed polices that concern anonymization, personally identifying information, and privacy:

- 47 of 50 policies made a distinction between "personally identifying information" and information that is "anonymized" and therefore not "personally identifying." Of those 47 policies, 22 made no attempt at all to explain the distinction.

- Of the remaining 25, 11 merely gave an incomplete list (e.g., "such as street address, phone number, email address…"). The remaining 14 made some attempt to explain what makes information "personally identifying."

- 10 of 50 policies explicitly stated that "anonymized" data sets were not treated as protected. None of the remaining 40 policies said that "anonymized" data would not be released.

- 24 of 50 policies either stated or implied that user data would be aggregated with data from other sources. No policy stated that this would not happen.

- 16 of 50 policies stated some reason why the company protected information.

- 14 of these 16 policies gave some variant of "You care about privacy and we want your business."

- Of the remaining 2, one stated that protecting privacy is a matter of "respect for the individual," and the other stated that doing so is a part of "fair information practices."

Nearly all of the policies surveyed made some type of distinction between "personally identifying" and "anonymized" data. Nearly half of those, however, did not explain how they defined the distinction—or exactly what protections were in place.

And the distinction is critical. Anonymized data is quickly becoming very difficult to maintain. And what constitutes "personally identifying" is matter of wide and variable opinion. To understand how to reduce the risks of inadvertent migration from one category to the other, organizations first have to understand what the risks are and the growing number of ways anonymized data sets can be aggregated and correlated quite easily to expose personally identifiable information.

An excellent primer here is Paul Ohm's "Broken Promises of Privacy" from the *UCLA Law Review* (2010; *http://papers.ssrn.com/sol3/papers.cfm?abstract_id=1450006*). In a nutshell, Ohm's point is this: for several decades, the foundation of information privacy law and practice has been the distinction between "personally identifying information" and other information.

Many of the policies reviewed explicitly state or clearly imply that "anonymized" data is not protected. However, whether a specific set of information (e.g., a street address or a set of ratings of content on a website) is "personally identifying" depends on what other information is available to someone trying to "reidentify" the people referenced in a data set (or "de-anonymize" the set).

For example, if someone doesn't know that you live at 312 Cherry Lane, then knowing that a package is going there doesn't associate the package with you. To someone lacking information correlating that street address with you, in that instance not even the street address is personally identifying.

Of course, data that connects street addresses to people is widely available. Ohm's point is that all sorts of data is available that makes it easy to aggregate and connect personal data with an individual person. The more such additional data is available (in addition to more easily accessible tools and computing resources), the easier it is to reattach supposedly "anonymous" data sets to canonical "personally identifying information" such as name, address, and phone number.

In one widely cited study, for instance, researchers were able to reidentify many users from an "anonymized" data set released by Netflix for the purposes of crowd-sourcing recommendation algorithms by comparing it to user profiles on IMDB (*http:// www.securityfocus.com/news/11497*).

You might not think that a few movie ratings could be "personally identifying information," but given the right auxiliary information, they are.

In the opening quote to this chapter, Ohm was talking specifically about the particular sense of the word "anonymous" that relates to an individual's personal privacy. But the reality is broader than that. Any context we create to turn data into information automatically assigns new characteristic to it, causing data *itself* to become less anonymous and more meaningful. And if we have enough data, we can correlate, extrapolate, query, or extract some very useful new information by understanding the relationships between those characteristics. The loss of data anonymity is a natural consequence of placing it in a context to create meaningful information. And while the value of that utility is growing exponentially in our time, so too is the unknown potential for unintended consequences of the many broad social and economic benefits derived from product and service innovations using big-data technologies.

This has serious repercussions for data-handling policies based on the personally identifying/anonymized distinction. Such policies can be implemented coherently only if there really is such a distinction, and Ohm argues rather persuasively that there isn't. As he puts it, "data can be either useful or perfectly anonymous, but never both" (*http:// papers.ssrn.com/sol3/papers.cfm?abstract_id=1450006*).

The broader implication is that as big data's forcing function grows larger and more powerful, more and more information may slip into the category of "personally identifying" in practice. If this is true, it means that the handling of personal data may become an activity with an increasingly large risk. Especially as business models based on aggregation and sharing "anonymized" data see their data transition into the "personally identifying" category.

That risk is manageable only to the degree that business models that rely on the use of "anonymized" data while seeking to protect "personally identifying" status can safely maintain the distinction. The policies of the Fortune 50 do little to promote confidence in their ability to maintain that distinction. Nearly half of all policies make no attempt at all to explain how they define "personally identifying" information. The rest either offer suggestive open-ended lists of the "name, address, and phone number…" variety or use vague circular phrases to illustrate the difference, such as "personally identifying information is information that can be traced back to a particular person."

The issue with such a vague formulation is that it provides no help in determining which information does not allow such "tracing back." Remember, the mere addition of a few IMDB movie reviews allowed researchers to identify specific individuals out of a supposedly "anonymized" set of data. In the face of growing evidence that aggregation is an increasingly powerful and available method of violating individual privacy, explicit ethical inquiry is a critical part of maintaining ethical coherence. A more mature understanding about what organizations value about privacy is needed. Either the business models that depend on the distinction between anonymized and personally identifying data need to be refined, or data-handling policies and procedures need to be developed that take account of the technological and conceptual problems with maintaining the distinction.

Data Ownership

At AT&T Labs in Florham Park, New Jersey, big data is being used to analyze the traffic and movement patterns of people through data generated by their mobile phones, to help improve policymaking and urban and traffic planning. The research team realized they could understand deep patterns of how people moved through urban environments by analyzing the flow of mobile devices from cell tower to cell tower. And they wanted to use those insights to help improve traffic flow and to inform better urban planning, not to improve their marketing.

But, of course, AT&T, along with Verizon, Google, TomTom, NAVTEQ, and several companies who help retail malls track the traffic patterns of shoppers, want very much to use that information to generate new streams of revenue. The question of privacy is top of mind (especially as the distinction between anonymized and personally identifying information becomes more difficult to maintain), but the question of ownership is equally compelling.

Since people buy their mobile devices, does the data generated by the use of those devices belong to the individual device owners—or to the company who owns and maintains the technological infrastructure that makes that usage possible?

The Electronic Frontier Foundation offers an interesting metaphor in response to this question:[3]

> "*Big data* is the mantra right now. Everyone wants to go there, and everyone has these stories about how it might benefit us," said Lee Tien, senior staff attorney with the Electronic Frontier Foundation, a San Francisco–based nonprofit organization specializing in free speech, privacy, and consumer rights.
>
> "One of the things you learn in kindergarten is that if you want to play with somebody else's toys, you ask them," Tien said. "What is distressing, and I think sad, about the big data appetite is so often it is essentially saying, 'Hey, we don't have to ask.'"

Google explicitly states that they "don't sell [their] user's personal information." However, they make no statement about who owns the information in the first place, which leaves the door wide open to allow them to utilize that information in their business model (notably the sale of online advertising) without denying or rejecting your claim to it.

And although Google very visibly provides information about how to "liberate" your data (*http://www.dataliberation.org/*), it has become common knowledge that the valuable services Google provides millions of people every day is paid for, at least in part, as a result of the implied (or *tacit*) agreement that Google can use some of the data created by your use of their products to generate revenue in their business model.

The question remains open, however, of the exact distinction between "personal information" and the set of all information that Google knows about you, which, when combined in the right way, could potentially expose enormous amounts of personal information. The tacit agreements we enter into as individuals with organizations who have access to vast amounts of personal data generate more risk than making those agreements explicit and easily understood and accessible.

Manifestation of Values

In many ways, an organization's business processes, technical infrastructure configuration, and data-handling procedures can be interpreted as a manifestation of their values.[4]

Seen this way, values are inherently expressed by these data-handling practices. Although it might not be completely possible to reverse-engineer a company's values by deconstructing their data-handling practices, it certainly is possible to learn more about what has been considered important enough to include by simply reading the policy statement.

---

3. *http://www.nj.com/news/index.ssf/2012/06/why_att_is_is_using_your_cell.html*

4. Thanks to Dion Hinchliffe for this intriguing insight.

And it is fair to assume that the absence of any particular consideration in the policy statement indicates that consideration was deemed not important enough to include. Without additional information, it's impossible to know exactly what was considered but ultimately not included or what those conversations were like. But we can know what ultimately did and did not make it into those statements, and infer some reasonable understanding of what the originating organization deems important.

Ethical Incoherence

Though many people hold privacy as a "right," and rising concerns about personal data usage frequently focus on perceived violations of this right, the majority of privacy policies themselves fail to address their value basis almost entirely. Only 2 of 50 policies stated any recognizably moral reason for having a privacy policy at all. Most polices said nothing, while a minority gave the nonmoral reason that people care about privacy and the company values their business.

This is important because it directly raises the question of how to close the gaps in data-driven business models to structure their activities in alignment with moral motives. Those who believe in "corporate social responsibility" would say there are recognizably moral reasons for business to act in alignment with their values. Others, such as Friedman famously (or perhaps infamously), have stated that corporations have responsibilities only to their shareholders—the implication being that any legal action that generates a profit is justified if it results in returning value to shareholders (*http://www.colo rado.edu/studentgroups/libertarians/issues/friedman-soc-resp-business.html*).

Regardless of where your organization falls on that spectrum, data-handling policies that reflect common values provide alignment benefits. And being more explicit about the value-based motivations for those policies, including any moral notion of a right to privacy, makes it easier to benefit from that alignment. So, whether the practice of providing an admittedly inconvenient method to opt out of the use of personal data for targeted advertising should continue can be answered by understanding why an organization has a privacy policy in the first place. If a company places greater value on providing increased individual control of the usage of personal data, then it's ethically incoherent to develop data-handling practices that make it difficult to opt out. If the intent of any specific policy is merely to reduce customer complaints and comply with the law, then reflecting actual values is immaterial. If the intent of the policy is to ensure that people's interests are respected, then simple opt-out procedures may be required to become ethically coherent.

A Policy By Any Other Name…

The vast majority of the Fortune 50 (46 out of 50) referred to the documents that explain their data-handling practices exclusively as "privacy" statements. The other aspects of big-data ethics (identity, ownership, and reputation) receive virtually no consideration in their current data-handling practices. Identity, ownership, and reputation would also benefit from more explicit consideration of how an organization's values inform their data-handling practices.

For example, there were virtually no discussions of what constitutes an "identity" in any of the reviewed policies. Even Google's new policies, previously separate across more than 60 different products, are now streamlined and integrated into one set of policy statements (effective March 1, 2012). They refer to them as "Privacy Policy" and "Terms of Service."

Although they explicitly define personal information as "information that you provide to us which personally identifies you, such as your name, email address or billing information, or other data which can be reasonably linked to such information by Google," there is no discussion of how they conceive of who *you* are—that is, what constitutes an *individual* identity. There is no clear definition of what a specific, individual, unique "you" to whom a name (what name?), email address, or billing information can be accurately assigned.

These actions imply that Google believes it is ethical for an organization to sell advertising based on data generated by people using their services as long as that data is not personally identifiable—according to their definition. This is a highly common practice, not only by Fortune 50 corporations, but the majority of business models using big data. And this practice carries with it substantial risk for at least two reasons:

- The high degree of variability between organizations. For example, what Google considers Personally Identifiable Information (PII) may be substantially different from Microsoft's definition. How are we to protect PII if we can't agree on what we're protecting?

- The increasing availability of open data (and increasing number of data breaches) that make cross-correlation and de-anonymization an increasingly trivial task. Let's not forget the example of the Netflix prize.

Finally, there is no mention anywhere, in any policy statement reviewed, no matter what it was called, that addressed the topic of reputation. Reputation might be considered an "aggregate" value comprised of personal information that is judged in one fashion or another. Again, however, this raises the question of what values an organization is motivated by when developing the constituent policies. Reputation is tied to an individual with a unique identity. Do the values we hold about that unique individual's privacy transfer completely to his reputation? What role do organizations play in protecting the data that might be used to assess a unique individual's reputation?

The complexity and accessibility of these policy statements is no minor concern either. In March 2012, Alexis Madrigal published an article in *The Atlantic* referencing a Carnegie Mellon research study that found it would require 76 working days to read all of the privacy policies we encounter (*http://www.theatlantic.com/technology/archive/2012/03/reading-the-privacy-policies-you-encounter-in-a-year-would-take-76-work-days/253851/*).

That is 76 working days for every one of us who agree to any policy whatsoever. Which is pretty much everyone. Imagine the economic impact if we all stopped working and chose to actually read all of them. If that happened, corporations would almost certainly find some value in making them less complex and more accessible.

Privacy is clearly of direct, relevant concern to everyone. However, the somewhat unsurprising time and cost associated with actually reading those policies represents a major opportunity for organizations to streamline communication of their position on the use of personal data.

A nice start would be to make a simple change: call them something else. Data Handling Policy, Usage Agreement, or Customer Protection Commitment all broaden the scope of what organizations can consider in their policy design in order to develop deeper engagement and build more trusting relationships with their market.

By explicitly including coverage of a broad range of concerns, organizations demonstrate proactive interest in recognizing the concerns of people who use their products and services. And reducing the long-form legalese format not only makes them more accessible, as research in *The Atlantic* article demonstrates, but decreasing the complexity has the added benefit of reducing the opportunity cost of learning exactly what is being done with all that data.

This isn't just about customer service. It is also about seizing an opportunity to benefit from aligning your organizational values with your actions. Both internal and external communication of which values are driving policy and action provide a range of benefits:

- Faster adoption by consumers by reducing fear of the unknown (how are you using my data?)
- Reduction of friction from legislation from a more thorough understanding of constrains and requirements
- Increased pace of innovation and collaboration derived from a sense of shared purpose generated by explicitly shared values
- Reduction in risk of unintended consequences from an overt consideration of long-term, far-reaching implications of the use of big-data technologies
- Brand value generated from leading by example

A simple change in the title and design of a "privacy policy" makes these benefits immediately available to both organizations and their customers or constituents. Taking an active interest in addressing concerns around identity, privacy, ownership, and reputation is low-cost, high-return way to build deeper brand engagement and loyalty.

In the absence of any clear best practice for how to communicate these values and how they drive business decisions (actions), we're left to wonder what data-handling practices an organization values at all.

Cultural Values

It is worth noting at this point that the majority of the Fortune 50 operates around the world. And there are a wide variety of values present in many of those other countries, cultures, and governments. And those values are reflected in their actions.

In Sweden, the FRA Law authorizes the Swedish government to tap all voice and Internet traffic that crosses its borders—without a warrant. It was met with fierce protests across the political spectrum (*http://en.wikipedia.org/wiki/FRA_law*). British privacy laws are a complex and complicated set of regulations that face serious challenges resulting from how people use platforms that rely on big data, such as Twitter (*http://www.huffington post.com/2011/05/23/uk-privacy-law-thrown-int_n_865416.html*). The number of closed-circuit television cameras (CCTV) in London is estimated to be almost two million (*http://en.wikipedia.org/wiki/Closed-circuit_television*). And it is well known that the Chinese government heavily regulates Internet traffic (*http://en.wikipedia.org/wiki/ Internet_censorship_in_the_People%27s_Republic_of_China*).

Just a few examples from only three countries show the wide variety of values at play in how technology in general, and big data in particular, are utilized and managed. The sheer variety itself shows how closely related values and actions are. And how those relationships show up is often demonstrated in our written policies, technical infrastructure, and data-handling practices and processes. There is significant value in understanding more fully how those policies, infrastructures, and practices are developed and managed.

So What Did We Learn?

It is clear that organizations are playing catch-up when it comes to understanding and articulating the values that drive their data-handling policies. There is a great deal of confusion about some critically important distinctions, such as what it means to be anonymized and what exactly "personally identifiable information" means, not to mention how to respond to the increasing difficulty of maintaining that distinction—whatever it turns out to be.

There are open questions about how to interpret existing policy statements in terms of what the originating organization values. In the absence of explicit and transparent statements and actions, policies inherently reflect value judgments, but in the vast majority of cases, it's unclear what those values are. The opportunity here is to build stronger brand engagement and customer loyalty.

The benefits of big-data innovation must be balanced by understanding the risks of unintended consequences. And organizations must be intentional about the inquiry. Identify and acknowledge gaps between values and actions, and make explicit plans to close them. Expand the domain of what is included in policy statements to include consideration for other key aspects of big-data ethics such as identity, ownership, and reputation. Actively seek to understand any hierarchy of values to help prioritize business decisions.

Along the way, you will learn to understand and appreciate the benefits offered by values-to-action alignment. The next chapter focuses on how to do just that.

CHAPTER 4

Aligning Values and Actions

I don't give advice. I can't tell anybody what to do.
Instead I say this is what we know about this
problem at this time. And here are the
consequences of these actions.

—Joyce Brothers

People don't buy what you do,
they buy why you do it.

—Simon Sinek

Methods and Tools

Ethics are highly conceptual and abstract, but the actions that you take to design and execute big-data innovations in business have very real consequences. Damage to your brand and customer relationships, privacy violations, running afoul of emerging legislation, and the possibility of unintentionally damaging reputations are all potential risks.

Big-data ethics stand in roughly the same relationship to organizational success as leadership and management: both are simultaneously abstract and highly influential in building and maintaining successful organizations. And both are deeply informed by values.

As detailed in previous chapters, ethical decision points can provide a framework and methodology for organizations to facilitate discussion about values and can help resolve conflicts about how to align actions with those values. In other words, they help align your tactical actions with your ethical considerations.

Learning how to recognize ethical decision points and developing an ability to generate explicit ethical discussions provide organizations with an operational capability that will be increasingly important in the future: the ability to demonstrate that business practices honor their values. This is, undoubtedly, not the only framework that can help, and it is also not a "magic bullet." Other organizational capabilities are required to support those business practices.

Fortunately, organizations already have many of those capabilities. Combined with traditional organizational capabilities—leadership and management, communication, education and training, process design and development, and strategic initiative development and execution—a responsible organization can use this alignment methodology to identify their values and execute on them.

These activities are more organic than strictly linear; ethical inquiry will interact with the analysis work. It may turn up insights that lead to a re-articulation of an organization's ethical position, while further analysis of those principles may uncover strengths or weaknesses in an organization's existing data-handling practices.

A responsible organization's goal is to identify, document, and then honor a common set of values by executing processes and business practices that are in alignment with those values. By combining existing skills and resources with this approach, organizations can grow their capacity to engage and manage any ethical challenges that big data generates.

But remember that it can be tempting to avoid the discussion entirely. And the politics of power in an organization can be complex to navigate. Roles including compliance or ethics might have the primary responsibility of making values and actions transparent, whereas other roles, such as legal or human resources, might be highly concerned with the implications of alignment failures. The tension there is not always easy to resolve. One purpose of the methods and tools described in this chapter is to introduce new ways to get the right people in the room to collaborate on resolving those tensions together.

Because ethics is an inherently personal topic, ethical discussions often expose conflicting values. To reduce the potential conflicts, it helps to focus on the common benefits that values-to-action alignment can bring—both to individuals and organizations. Operational efficiency, the reduction of risk, creating space for individual contributions, and stronger external relationships with partners and customers are all benefits that derive from clarity of the values that drive the execution of organizational action.

In framing up workshops or other meetings for these discussions, the strongest source of motivating participation, regardless of the role, is to help drive innovation. The rapid pace of changing market conditions, in nearly every sector of the economy, is making innovation one of the most powerful competitive tools available. Some even argue that innovation is the *primary* driver of economic value (*http://blogs.valvesoftware.com/abrash/valve-how-i-got-here-what-its-like-and-what-im-doing-2/*).

And, while focusing on innovation can be a risky business, the desire to help others reduce that risk and create new economic value is often a deeply held personal value. Finding the common ground for entering into ethical discussions is often half the battle. It is frequently a matter of asking the right question or framing the inquiry in the most accessible way. In most cases, if you ask people what they want, it turns out they will tell you. So when faced with resistance to participating in or using these methods and tools, seek out the needs and goals of the individuals who can contribute to the discussion. Understanding the common purpose will reduce a significant amount of resistance and dissolve a wide variety of tensions.

Even then, however, it's not always easy to navigate the complexities of organizational politics. And although these methods and tools can be used by anyone, at any level of the organization, it is often helpful to have a neutral third-party facilitator or to engage an outside perspective or resource to help identify landmarks and pitfalls. In either case, the goal is to just start the discussion. The best practice is to consider it an ongoing process, not a singular event. There may be one or more discrete activities (workshops, meetings, discussions, etc.), but when taken together and viewed in the context of the framework, those activities form a new organizational capability that is becoming increasingly important.

The ecosystem of activities can be viewed as a "virtuous circle" of influence that can be entered at any point, is informed by the findings and insight of the previous set of activities, and subsequently informs the work in the next set. It is worth noting that this methodology is not strictly a checklist. Although there are discrete sets of activities, they influence and inform each other as they unfold.

This methodology is not intended to tell you what is ethical for you or your organization. Circumstances, culture, market, economic conditions, organization size and purpose, and a vast array of other factors make it very difficult to develop a common set of values that would work well in all contexts. Even current efforts to create a "digital bill of rights" or "data-handling manifesto" struggle to be relevant and directive enough to inform specific action. They are also open to wide interpretation. This methodology gives you some tools to get very specific about your values and how to align them with very tactical actions that are directly relevant to your highly specific context. It is a place to start.

Alignment Methodology Framework

As briefly introduced in Chapter 2, the four core components are: Inquiry, Analysis, Articulation, and Action.

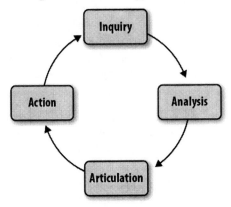

Alignment Methodology Framework

Inquiry
> Discovery and discussion of core organizational values

Analysis
> Review of current data-handling practices and an assessment of how well they align with core organizational values

Articulation
> Explicit, written expression of alignment and gaps between values and practices

Action
> Tactical plans to close alignment gaps that have been identified and to encourage and educate how to maintain that alignment as conditions change over time

Inquiry

The foundation of ethical inquiry stems from a basic understanding of whether actions and business practices are aligned with values by first exploring exactly what those values are. Because big data's forcing function interacts with a broad spectrum of your customers' lives, the subsequent range of values it can influence is equally broad, and it can be hard, messy work to uncover a foundational set of values more meaningful than mere platitudes.

While a mission or organizational values statement can serve as a guide for an organization's purpose, ethical inquiry seeks to understand the set of fundamental values that drive subsequent organizational action. The outcome of which is an understanding and articulation of those values that is more detailed and nuanced than a traditional mission statement.

To help get to a place where those values are being discussed authentically, here are some opening questions:

- Are people entitled to know how their data is used in the business?

- Are people entitled to know which organization holds their data and what data in particular it holds?

- Are people entitled to know how their data is analyzed and how the results of these analyses drive the business?

- Are people entitled to know who within the organization has access to the data?

- Are people entitled to know to what third parties the data is transferred (sold, given, released publicly, etc.)? If so, is it the organization's responsibility to let those people know what these third parties will do with the data? (That is, is it the originating organization's responsibility or a receiving organization's further down the data trail?)

- To the extent that people do have the previously listed entitlements, what constitutes sufficient notice to them of the relevant facts? May they be buried in long End-User License Agreements (EULA) that few people will read?[1] Must those entitlements or license agreements be explained clearly in everyday language, or is it the responsibility of the end users to distill the legal language into something they can understand?

- In general, should data collection occur through an opt-in or an opt-out model? Should other things, such as long-term storage or transfer to third parties, be opt-in or opt-out?

- What data raises the most organizational risk? What is required to determine the risk-benefit ratio of not collecting that data?

- Do data-handling practices generate external influences that specific values demand not be created? (Examples could be social networks diminishing real-world relationships or music recommendation services reducing the ability to make discerning judgments.)

---

1. As mentioned, it has recently been noted to that reading all the EULA you encounter would take an entire month every year (*http://www.techdirt.com/articles/20120420/10560418585/to-read-all-privacy-policies-you-encounter-youd-need-to-take-month-off-work-each-year.shtml*). The full study is here: *http://lorrie.cranor.org/pubs/readingPolicyCost-authorDraft.pdf.*

- Do data storage practices—even if the data collection involves infringing on no particular ethical values—create a resource that would be of use to powerful negative forces in the world, such as malicious or misguided governmental organizations, organized crime, or nefarious hackers? Is a responsible organization acting unethically if it does not have a definitive perspective on this question?

At least a preliminary set of answers to these types of questions will help identify what values you hold and begin to uncover what data-handling actions you make in accordance with those values.

It is preferable to start with the general and move toward the specific—to the degree of precision and articulation your unique circumstances allow. And they may not allow for much. Given an expectation that data-handling practices and values may evolve over time in response to changes in market dynamics, technology innovations, or broad changes in strategic business direction, they do not need to be carved in stone. It is sufficient at this stage to express these values as a set of general guidelines.

Ethical decisions are complex by their very nature, and perspectives and opinions vary widely among individuals. They vary even more when organizational imperatives from management, investors, or the marketplace (e.g., demands to operate profitably) are included in the mix. And this is precisely why an explicit and focused exploration of a shared set of common values is useful.

That said, the motivation isn't "we should explore values because it's difficult." The motivation is that you should explore them because big-data technologies are offering you an opportunity to operate in more beneficial ways and to generate more value in doing so: ways that apply to individuals, organizations, and society at large as the result of maintaining a healthy and coherent balance between risk and innovation—and between values and actions.

Those benefits were mentioned in Chapter 2, but are worth highlighting here. Specifically:

Reduction of risk of unintended consequences

An explicit articulation of a shared set of common values isn't going to answer every possible future question for working teams. But this articulation will significantly reduce the amount of overhead discussion required to develop an action plan in response to an event.

Increase in team effectiveness

A shared set of common values reduces operational friction in precisely the same way a political initiative or social cause benefits from the shared beliefs of its members. When designing products and services using big data, even a general, preliminary agreement about what's OK and what's not among team members greatly improves a communal ability to focus on solving problems—rather than conducting an ethical debate about which problems to solve.

Increased alignment with market and customer values

The business benefits of acknowledging and explicitly articulating organizational values and how they align with customers derive from the same increase in cohesion as shared values in internal teams. People who value the same things often work better together. Organizations who understand their customer or constituent's values are better able to meet them—resulting in greater customer satisfaction and deeper, more meaningful brand engagement.

As we saw in Chapter 3, however, values and actions are deeply intertwined.

Consider your own actions in daily life. They are, in part, motivated by your values. Perhaps some not as deeply as others, and there are often trade-offs to be made and balances to be maintained. People who value sustainable lifestyles may nonetheless choose to drive to work in order to support their basic need to generate income. Seeking an acceptable balance, they may elect only to ride bicycles on the weekend. Eating a healthy diet or exercising aligns with personal health values.

In every case, however, making those trade-offs and maintaining that balance is impossible without first understanding, explicitly and authentically, what values are in play. And the broad influence of big data's forcing function is widening the scope of inquiry every day.

Analysis

The goal of ethical inquiry is to develop an understanding of organizational values. The next step, analysis, is to determine how well actual data-handling practices are in alignment with them. This analysis can be more complex for an established organization than it is for a proposed startup (which typically do not, it is fair to assume, have mature plans for unintended consequences or employee failures to act in accordance with company policy).

Big-data startups can exploit an advantage here. By understanding core values in advance of building out their operational processes and technology stack, they can actually take action to build their values directly into their infrastructure. In some ways, an organization's technology configuration, business processes, and data-handling practices can be viewed as a physical manifestation of their values.

General topic themes are a good start. As a reminder, many organizations already have mature business capabilities that can contribute much to inquiry and analysis. Compliance, human resources, legal, finance and accounting, data architecture, technology and product planning, and marketing all have unique and informed perspectives.

Consider the specific examples: discussed next: data-handling audits and data-handling practices.

Data-handling audit

A key task in the evaluation of your current practices is a thorough audit of data-handling practices. A wide variety of organizational or business units touch many aspects of data handling. A rigorous audit will include process owners from each business group involved in any aspect of how data is handled. Considerations include:

- Who within your organization has access to customer data?
- Are they trustworthy?
- By what methods have you determined them to be trustworthy?
- What processes are in place to ensure that breaches of trust will be noticed?
- What technical security measures are taken with data?
- Are they sufficient for the purposes?
- Who outside of your organization might be interested in gaining access to the data you hold?
- How strong is their interest, and what means might be at their disposal to breach your security?

A responsible organization will conduct a thorough audit aimed at answering such questions. Traditional workshop and audit tools and processes can be useful in this work.

Process maps
> A data ethics audit team will benefit from a process diagram and associated task lists for how data is acquired, processed, secured, managed, and used in products and services.

Facilitated workshops
> It is far more efficient and more likely to uncover gaps and overlaps in data-handling practices by gathering a core team together to work through a series of audit exercises. These exercises should be designed to discover and explore the ways in which organizational values are—or are not—being honored in data-handling practices.

One-on-one focus interviews
> This activity is best used to supplement facilitated workshops and to uncover more candid concerns about values-actions alignment. Focus interviews are aimed at discovering how people handle data, the extent to which they understand and share the organization's values, and whether those practices contain any weaknesses.

Security reviews
> There is an entire field of expertise and discipline centered on information technology security. A responsible organization utilizes experts in this field to generate a deep understanding of their data security systems and practices.

Attack scenarios

Facilitated exercises to explore and imagine various attack scenarios can generate massive insights into how well existing data handling practices would stand up to specific efforts to access customer data. These exercises are most successfully conducted in a cross-functional group where visual thinking and collaborative problem solving are key tools. Executed well, gaps and overlaps in data-handling practices can be uncovered quickly and efficiently.

Aggregation audits

There is a growing realization that personal information can, in unfavorable circumstances, be the missing link needed by someone who intends to do harm by connecting people to information that may have an ethical impact.[2] A responsible organization will ask itself under what conditions their customer information would actually be useful to anyone seeking to correlate previously disaggregated data sets—whether with the intention of doing harm or not.

Risk/harm scenarios

What sorts of harm can your organizational data do—either by itself, if exposed, or by correlating or aggregating with any other imaginable data set? This question might be more easily answered if you run an anonymous offshore social network for dissidents in an authoritarian country and more difficult to answer if you run a site for local music reviews.

Here is a clear example of where inquiry and analysis are deeply intertwined. If organizational values support a strict and 100% anonymous ability to connect and communicate with other people, it is natural to imagine that organization's data-handling practices will support those values by implementing extremely rigorous security and other handling procedures.

Internal conflicts

Individuals can certainly hold views that conflict with organizational values. While the broader purpose of the entire cycle of Inquiry, Analysis, Articulation, and Action is intended to align values and actions both internally and externally, understanding where individual and organization values conflict (or are out of alignment) is key to closing those gaps. Value Personas, discussed later in this chapter, are a useful tool to facilitate this understanding and alignment.

---

2. *http://arstechnica.com/tech-policy/2009/09/your-secrets-live-online-in-databases-of-ruin/*

Surveys

Online surveys of customers or internal teams are also useful at this phase, with the understanding of the natural strengths and limitations of surveys generally. Survey responses may be a result of misinformation or misunderstanding of what an organization actually does with customer data. It may be difficult to craft the right questions on such conceptual and nuanced topics. Surveys are, however, a well-established research mechanism to gather large amounts of information in a short period of time and are a valuable arrow in the data ethics audit quiver.

Data-handling practices

The promise of benefits from big-data innovation needs to be balanced by the potential risk of negative impact on identity, privacy, ownership, or reputation. In order to maintain that balance, organizations must understand their *actual* data-handling practices —not what they think they are or what an outdated process diagram says they are. This requires a thorough consideration of how those practices influence each aspect of big-data ethics: identity, privacy, ownership, and reputation.

For a responsible organization, this is not a matter of an arbitrary "what if?" session. It is a matter of gathering real, accurate information about any methods or resources that might expose information about which there are ethical implications—and the likelihood of this happening.

The goal is to take a clear look at what is done with data within the organization and to describe the actual practices (not merely the intended or perceived ones) accurately so as to facilitate rigorous analysis. An open, inclusive approach including all relevant personnel will provide greater insight into the sensitivity of the data one's organization holds. Consider the extent to which any single individual may ordinarily be unaware of the details of the data process that drive the implementation of their business model. Including cross-functional roles in this discussion helps to expose and close any gaps in any one individual's understanding and generates a more robust and complete picture of the operational reality.

The complexity of targeted advertising is a prime example, not to mention a likely familiar use case to many businesses. It is a complex business activity typically involving multiple individuals and technologies within an organization, close data-sharing partnerships with other organizations, multiple web properties, and dozens (or possibly hundreds) of content producers and consumers. This complexity raises familiar issues of third-party usage of personal data, privacy, ownership, and a growing realization that major big-data players often are not entirely transparent about how their applications are interacting with your data.

For example, in February 2012, the *New York Times* reported on news that the mobile social networking application "Path" was capturing and storing ostensibly private information (contact information on mobile devices, such as names, phone numbers, etc.) without notifying people (*http://bits.blogs.nytimes.com/2012/02/12/disruptions-so-many-apologies-so-much-data-mining/*).

The resulting responses ranged from ethical comments (from the *Guardian*: "It's not wrong to store someone's phone contacts on a server. It's wrong to do it without telling them"[3]) to the realization mentioned in the article that the mere location of data influenced how much protection the First Amendment could actually provide.

Banner ads are a common targeted advertisement technique, and many people strongly dislike seeing banner ads for products based on their browsing history—especially when those advertisements seem irrelevant. Some might argue that since people are going to see *some* ad, it might as well be a targeted one because even poorly targeted advertising based on browsing history is bound to be of more interest to consumers than ads published merely at random. Yet the practice, even when entirely automated, still raises the suspicion that third parties know where they have been browsing specific content and then passing that information to others for a fee.

Targeted advertising today is maturing and improving accuracy at a rapid pace. But there are still potentially negative consequences based on the perception that there is something wrong with it. In February 2012, the *Wall Street Journal* reported that Google was embedding software on some websites to circumvent a default setting on Safari web browsers in order to target advertising (*http://online.wsj.com/article_email/SB10001424052970204880404577225380456599176-lMyQjAxMTAyMDEwNjExNDYyWj.html#articleTabs%3Darticle*). Google responded with a statement that said their intention was benign and they did not collect any personal information. The Federal Trade Commission (FTC) responded with an investigation. In July of 2012, Bloomberg reported that the fine is expected to be a record $22.5 million (*http://www.bloomberg.com/article/2012-07-10/a4ZIufbs2jko.html*).

The message is clear: a responsible organization must decide for itself how far it must extend its data-handling practices in order to honor its values. The complete data exhaust trail of big data can reach dozens, even hundreds, of other organizations. A thorough understanding of which third parties have access to your organization's data (through sales, storage, sharing, or any other means) must be developed and documented up to and including the point your values dictate.

3. *http://www.guardian.co.uk/technology/appsblog/2012/feb/09/path-privacy-apps*

Considerations include:

- With whom do you share your data?
- Is it sold to third parties? If so, what do they do with it, and to whom do they in turn sell it?
- Do you release it publicly at times? If so, how strong are your anonymization procedures?
- Who might be motivated to de-anonymize?
- Who might partially de-anonymize by correlating your data with other data?
- How likely would any aggregation lead to harm?

Answering these questions requires a thorough understanding of the sorts of correlation, aggregation, and de-anonymization that are possible with your customers' data, and likelihood and the possible motives others may have to do so. (*http://www.schneier.com/blog/archives/2010/03/de-anonymizing.html*). Data sharing, whether intentional or inadvertent, requires a thorough knowledge of the data landscape and technical issues of a wide variety of aggregation possibilities, paired with the sociological, psychological, and economic factors relevant to understanding their potential actions.

For example, third parties with access to customer data may be hesitant to share information about their own practices, citing a variety of constraints such as competitive intelligence, intellectual property, or their own value system. While this hesitation itself is not sufficient cause for concern, a responsible organization may honor its values by inquiring whether third-party data-handling practices align with their own.

Analysis at this stage should also include consideration for any long-term external effects data-handling practices might have—especially those with ethical implications. How would widespread adoption of your product or service affect the quality of people's lives? In order to discover the extent of those implications, it helps to get informed opinions from a broad array of existing functional areas in the business, especially those familiar with your particular business model.

There may also be external implications from either the long-term effects or the large-scale use of available data. Exploring these implications requires consideration of relevant principles in a wide variety of areas: finance, marketing, data security, law, market conditions and economics, and social psychology. As data sharing extends beyond organizational boundaries and control, a broad range of factors may affect operational processes in actual practice. A responsible organization may find that the data exhaust trail of their data practices has surprisingly far-reaching consequences.

The outcome of inquiry and analysis activities is dependent on many factors.

Considerations include:

- Type of organization
- Roles and responsibilities of the participants
- Duration and complexity of the process
- Complexity of the data ecosystem and technology stack
- Industry or market of operation

These considerations, and many others specific to your particular circumstances, will all influence the format and content of the results. And this variety of outcomes is to be expected. No two businesses are exactly alike, and no two organizations' values systems and subsequent actions are likely to be identical either. Generalities and comparisons can often be made, but the circumstances under which ethical values inform your organizational actions are unique.

Generally, however, inquiry and analysis activities result in a set of findings and insights captured in document or visual form, such as:

- Provisional statement of organizational principles
- Security audit findings
- Data-handling processes and polices (in written and visual form)
- Documents describing the sensitivity, use, and sharing of held data
- Insights into practices of similar organizations (industry norms)
- External implications and current insights and perceptions on their degree of risk
- Gaps and overlaps in values-actions alignment

Articulation

The goal of Articulation is to answer this (admittedly difficult) question: are your organization's practices (actions) in alignment with its stated principles (values) or not?

On the one hand, inquiry and analysis may demonstrate that the set of identified values needs revision. On the other hand, the organization's values may be found to be basically acceptable to the organization as they stand, and current data handling practices found wanting and requiring adjustment.

The tools that are available to articulate values-to-action alignment are:

- Ethical principles in the form of value statements (the results of Inquiry)
- Explicit analysis and documentation of existing practices (the results of Analysis)

Based on previous inquiry and analysis, a wide variety of possible scenarios might be uncovered. Security may be insufficient given the sensitivity of held data. A specific data collection process may be out of alignment with certain values. Refusal of third parties with access (either paid or not) to data sets to describe their own practices may warrant discontinuation of business with those third parties.

The goal of these activities is to generate and express an agreement about what an organization is going to do—that is, what actions it will take in alignment with which values.

Your organization can move from the highly conceptual, abstract nature of values and ethics to a useful and tactical action plan by identifying gaps (misalignment between values and actions) and articulating how you intend to gain and maintain alignment.

Inquiry and analysis will inform this articulation, and discussions across the organization, including as many viewpoints and perspectives as possible, can provide additional insight on existing and evolving practices. The intention is to *generate explicit discussion*. Books, articles, emerging legislation, news reports, and blog entries on existing norms and practices for your industry or of similar organizations are a rich source of generating a comprehensive, comparative view of data-handling practices.

Action

To implement those actions, a Value Persona (explained in the next section) can be a helpful planning tool. And you're now in familiar territory: running programs and projects, setting and tracking milestones, and measuring performance against defined benchmarks. Value Persona worksheets can help you discover a wealth of information about how your organization intends to navigate ethical waters and can be used in parallel with more familiar tools, including project and action plans, communication plans, improved business processes, education programs, or revised hiring strategies.

Some examples of ethical decision points where a Value Persona might be useful:

- Adding a single new feature
- Policy development
- Security breaches
- Designing an entirely new product
- Designing an entirely new set of product features

- Opportunity to benefit from combining two distinct data sets

Value Personas

As a tool to help aid in the articulation of those values and the subsequent organizational actions, Value Personas offer a means for facilitating discussion about organizational alignment in actions, business practices, and individual behaviors based on a common set of values. They contain a description of key roles, any ethical decision points, alignment actions, and anticipated outcomes. They help to identify shared values and create a vocabulary for explicit dialog, thereby reducing risk from misalignment and encouraging collaboration and innovation across working teams.

The use of audience (or user) personas is a common methodology in advertising, user experience design, and product and market research. In traditional practice, attributes are associated with a hypothetical individual for the purpose of segmenting audiences into predictable behaviors and needs.

Value Personas are an evolution of traditional user personas that express how a specific value shows up and influences action within an organization. Value Personas shed light on moments when the use of big-data technologies raises an ethical (or value-focused) decision point. A Value Persona can suggest options for how to align shared values with proposed action from various organizational role perspectives.

Value Personas are developed using persona worksheets. The worksheets provide a working space for notes, drawings, sketches, illustrations, and remarks as teams work through the details of building an effective action plan to achieve alignment.

Value Personas provide a means for framing up explicit ethical inquiry and are highly flexible and amendable to many given contexts.

They assume several things:

- First, values do not take action; people do. It is only through action that values show up. And, as discussed earlier, your values are inherent in your actions all the time. The benefit of the Value Persona is to identify and document which values are showing up in your actions—and how.

- Second, values can be intentionally aligned with actions. Although it is true that an individual or an organization can hold conflicting values—which can result in conflicting actions—the Value Persona can help make those conflicts transparent.

- Finally, values are not ethics. Ethics are derived from values. Ethics are expressions of which actions are valued and which are not. Values are a measurement of whether those actions are ethical. The Value Persona is the stick by which ethical alignment can be measured.

VALUE PERSONA WORKSHEET   A TOOL FOR ALIGNING VALUES & ACTIONS

Use this worksheet to create alignment between values and actions. Start with any ethical decision point and its associated values. Identify the possible actions for each organizational role involved in making the decision. Through discussion, agree on the actions which are most aligned with your values. Then describe the desired outcomes of those actions: both internal and external. Use completed worksheets to inform tactical action plans.

[1] DESCRIBE ETHICAL DECISION POINT
Any decision in which alignment between values and actions is desired.

[2] DESCRIBE THE RELEVANT VALUE(S) OF YOUR BUSINESS
The values inherent in the ethical decision point.

[3] LIST POTENTIAL ACTIONS FOR EACH ROLE	[4] HOW DOES THIS ALIGN WITH OUR VALUES?	[5] CHOOSE ACTION(S)	[6] LIST DESIRED OUTCOMES
What could be done about it? Consider all options from passive to active.	What's the degree of alignment with the business value(s) for each outcome? Reassess potential actions if needed.	Select those actions which are most aligned with the values in question.	Describe the impact of each action **internally and externally.**
ROLE: POTENTIAL ACTIONS:	NOT ALIGNED — VERY ALIGNED		
ROLE: POTENTIAL ACTIONS:	NOT ALIGNED — VERY ALIGNED		
ROLE: POTENTIAL ACTIONS:	NOT ALIGNED — VERY ALIGNED		
ROLE: POTENTIAL ACTIONS:	NOT ALIGNED — VERY ALIGNED		

If an organization values transparency, changing their data-handling policy without notifying anyone means it is not acting in alignment with its values. A slightly more difficult example is how to honor the value of transparency in the event of an unexpected security breach. Should a responsible organization be *completely* transparent and notify everyone, should it be transparent just to the individuals whose data was breached, or should it extend that transparency to those organizations who would be affected down the data exhaust trail? How far does the value of transparency extend?

Imagine an opportunity to add a new product feature based on the correlation of two distinct data sets that allows more finely grained customer segmentation. But it comes at the cost of combing data sets from two different companies with two different policies about how their customer data can be used. It can be difficult to see how to maintain alignment across a range of multiorganizational values while simultaneously benefiting from that innovation. In some cases, those values will not conflict. In other cases, they may. Even identifying when they will and when they won't can be a full-time job—let alone determining an appropriate course of action.

Value Personas can help parse out the conflicts between what you value and how you should act based on those values. They provide a mechanism for developing a common vocabulary, based on and informed by your own personal moral codes and aimed toward developing a set of common, shared values, which help reduce organizational barriers to productivity and encourage collaboration and innovation.

Some Value Personas may live essentially intact and unchanged for long periods. Others may evolve regularly based on changes in market conditions, new technologies, legislation, prevailing common practices, or evolutions in your business model. The dynamics of the conditions around which business decisions are made are highly variable and subject to influences that are often difficult to anticipate. Value Personas reduce the need to anticipate every possible outcome by treating them as worksheets capable of being used, revised, updated, and discarded as needed in response to those changes.

Turning discussion into action

Technologists work constantly to evolve the abilities of big data. Social norms and legislation are slower to evolve. Competitive market forces, depending on your industry, can change at many different rates, from instantly to quarterly or yearly. There is no reason to expect that your ability to maintain alignment between your values and your actions can be wholly articulated fully in advance of all business conditions. Indeed, one of the benefits of the innovation opportunities big data provides is that it allows organizations to rapidly adjust to these market and competitive forces.

The ability to align values with actions allows organizations to create a common and shared sense of purpose and action around any given business initiative. As previously mentioned, turning the question of "*should* we do this" into "how *can* we do this" unleashes more collaborative thinking and work.

Value Personas, as a tool for developing this capability, are inherently scalable. Full, multiday workshops can provide ample time for organizations to develop a mature realization of their values and articulate suggested actions at various ethical decision points. However, these methods and tools works equally well in ad hoc hallway or working meeting conversations where ethical questions suddenly arise and ethical discussions begin.

Ideally, your organization has a core set of values to provide a starting point for these less formal use cases, but even in the face of disagreement about foundational values, Value Personas can give people a tool to start productive conversations.

Those conversations become productive when they're made transparent and explicit. Value Personas can help as a tool, but the goal is not a nicely filled out worksheet. The goal is a clear and distinct plan of action, taking into account each individual role involved, and articulating exactly what each person is going to do, in what order, and what the intended outcomes or goals are for each action.

Global Data Management: A Case Study

Consider the fictional company Global Data Management, a B2B data-handling and transaction processing company that explicitly values transparency in their data-handling practices. They publicly publish that position, actively share detailed information about their business operations, and frequently update their business strategy based on direct feedback from their customers. They share this information via many different communication channels, including: Twitter, their online customer community, blog posts, regular press releases, and their annual report. They have become very good at communicating with their customers. They have solid, long-term relationships with a large percentage of their customer base, and that base is growing in low double-digit percentages each quarter.

Global Data Management uses big-data technology to provide the majority of the products and services it offers. They run a Hadoop cluster of nearly 100 machines, process near real-time analytics reporting with Pentaho, and are experimenting with ways to enhance their customers' ability to analyze their own datasets using R for statistical analysis and graphics. Their combined customer data sets exceed 100 terabytes and are growing daily.

Further, they are especially excited about a powerful new opportunity their data scientists have uncovered that would integrate some of the data in *their customers'* databases with *other* customer data to enhance and expand the value of the services they offer for everyone.

They are aware, however, that performing such correlations must be done in a highly secure environment, and a rigorous test plan is designed and implemented. During the process of testing this new cross-correlated customer data set innovation, a security breach occurs. Global Data Management is devastated. A disgruntled employee, who had legitimate access to the data, walked out of the data center with a hard drive onto which he had copied tens of thousands of records of Global Data Management's customers' personal banking and financial transaction histories of *their* customers.

Now Global Data Management is faced with not just legal but also ethical questions. Their legal obligation may be to their customers only, but do their ethical obligations extend beyond those legal requirements? This scenario of unintended consequences generates a specific values-actions alignment question about the extent of notification required.

That is, does their value of transparency extend to their customers' customers?

The ethical decision point can be framed in several different ways:

- Do they tell just their customers, or do they have an obligation to tell their customers' customers, too?
- How far do they extend their value of transparency?
- Does transparency mean "anyone who might be affected," or does it just mean "those who are directly affected by our actions?"

There are likely to be several organizational roles involved in this ethical inquiry. Examples may include the CEO or COO, a representative from human resources, the data center manager, the manager of the disgruntled employee in question, and perhaps a representative from legal. These individuals bring both their own personal moral codes and their professional expertise to the inquiry.

This fictional example of a Value Persona shows the results of a productive discussion about how to align various proposed actions with Global Data Management's value of transparency.

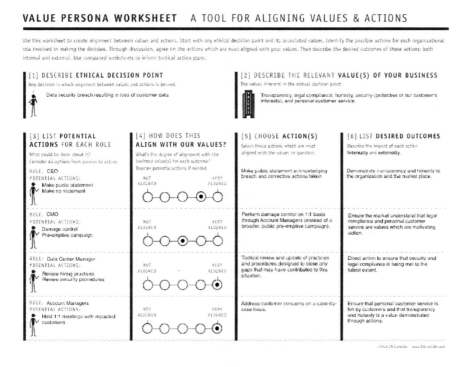

Used in this way, a Value Persona creates a common vision for guiding organizational practice that aligns with organizational principle.

Value Personas are a tool for implementing strategic decisions in a business practice. They express a clear statement of how a set of shared values is to be realized in the execution of business operations. They are most useful when shared throughout the organization and when everyone understands how, when, and where to apply them.

One of the best mechanisms for communicating those statements is derived from visual thinking exercises, which can result in many different formats and outcomes. One popular artifact is a detailed "usage map," which is a visual representation of value-action gaps and the tactical steps that will be taken to close them. Usage maps can be highly engaging and visually depict a course of action that is easily shared across an organization to help facilitate common understanding.

Benefits of Alignment

When organizational practices and processes (actions) are aligned to support a comprehensive and explicit statement of principles (values), the benefits are many.

Employees, partners, owners, and so forth can collect their wages and profits in good conscience. Organizations can expect to enjoy better press coverage, better relations with customers and other generators of personal data, and quite likely increased revenues as individuals and organizations that previously avoided doing business together due to concerns with its handling of data come to view it as an organization that handles personal data in a responsible manner.

This doesn't mean that all problems will disappear: disagreements over values can be heated and difficult to resolve. Individual moral codes are hard-won through life experience and they can be a challenge to evolve. But significant benefit can be realized from widely communicating Value Personas and the action plans they inform across an organization to help align operations and values in a consistent and coherent way.

Big data is one of, if not the, most influential technological advancement in our lifetime. The forcing function big data exerts on our individual and collective lives extends, and will continue to expand, into ever more personal and broadly influential aspects of society, politics, business, education, healthcare, and undoubtedly new areas we haven't even thought of yet.

Businesses using big data now have to make strategic choices about how to share their innovations and balance them against the risk of exposing too much of their unique value proposition, thereby opening them up to competitive forces in their markets. The judicial system, from the Supreme Court on down, is now actively making legal judgments about everything from consumer protection and how big data is influencing personal privacy, to Constitutional issues ranging from First Amendment protections of free speech to Fourth Amendment rights against unreasonable search and seizure.

Politicians and governmental leaders from US Presidential candidates to the entire long-standing government of Hosni Mubarak in Egypt have experienced the power and influence of the ability of great masses of people, with a set of shared and common values and purpose, to change the course of history using simple tools such as social networks and Twitter.

Today, examples of social change and communication are available everywhere. Greenpeace has dozens of Twitter accounts organized by country and almost a half-million followers on one global account. Actor Ashton Kutcher can reach over 10 million people instantly. The American Red Cross has over 700 thousand followers. One has to wonder what Martin Luther King, Jr. would have done with a Twitter account. Or how the Civil War would have been changed in a world with blogs and real-time search. The telegraph was instrumental enough in how wartime communication took place; what if Lincoln or Churchill and Roosevelt had instant messaging? The Occupy movement has benefited enormously from being able to coordinate action and communicate its message on the backs of big-data systems. And, at both ends of the spectrum, imagine a data breach at Facebook: what would Hitler have done with that information? How would Mahatma Gandhi have utilized that kind of information about so many people?

And because of the sheer velocity, volume, and variety of big data, as it evolves, it is introducing ethical challenges in places and ways we've never encountered before. To meet those challenges in those new and unexpected ways, we simply must learn to engage in explicit ethical discussion in new and unexpected environments—not only to protect ourselves from the risk of unintended consequences, but because there are legitimate and immediate benefits.

The evolution of what it means to have an identity, both on and offline, raises deeply important questions for the future. If identity is prismatic, as Chris Poole suggests, do each of the aspects of our identity have equal rights? Are we to be allowed to change different aspects equally? Similar ethical questions exist around privacy. For an in-depth look at these questions, see *Privacy and Big Data* by Terence Craig and Mary E. Ludloff (O'Reilly).

Similarly, what it means to actually own something is changing. Do we own our personal data? If so, how do property rights extend (or not) to the use of personal data in exchange for products and services? What will be considered a fair and accurate judgment of an individual's reputation in the future? Is an individual's complete history of actions and behaviors on the Internet useful in making hiring decisions? There are certainly some companies who think so and will provide you with that information in exchange for a fee.

But even in the face of all these questions, the opportunity to extract value while reducing the risks is too tempting to ignore. Longitudinal studies in education hold the promise of helping us learn how to teach more effectively. Healthcare is running at mach speed to understand diseases and the human genome, and to improve doctor and hospital performance. Explicit ethical inquiry makes it easier to honor emerging and evolving legislation. As the law changes, understanding individual and organizational values (and how they relate to each other) and the actions they motivate will decrease the amount of time it takes to figure out how to be in compliance.

The alignment of common values and actions serves to increase the pace of innovation and make working teams incredibly more productive and efficient. Internal and external alignment deepens brand engagement with customers and generates loyalty and higher rates of satisfaction.

And so this book advocates not only learning how to engage in explicit ethical inquiry, but also suggests several tools and approaches for doing so. A practice of engaging in ethical dialog contributes to a much stronger ability to maintain a balance between the risk of unintended consequences and the benefits of innovation. We hope that those tools and approaches are helpful in your efforts to develop, engage in, and benefit from explicit ethical inquiry.

About the Authors

Kord Davis is a former Principal Consultant with Cap Gemini and has spent nearly 20 years providing business strategy, analysis, and technical consulting to over 100 organizations of all sizes including: Autotask, Microsoft, Intel, Sisters of Mercy Healthcare, Nike, Bonneville Power Administration (BPA), Northwest Energy Alliance (NEEA), Bill & Melinda Gates Foundation, Western Digital, Fluke, Merix, Roadway Express, and Gardenburger. Integrating a professional background in telecommunications and an academic background in philosophy, he brings passionate curiosity, the rigor of analysis, and a love of how technology can help us do the things we really want to do better, faster, and easier. A formally trained workgroup facilitator, he holds a BA in Philosophy from Reed College and professional certifications in communication, systems modeling, and enterprise transformation.

Have it your way.

Get even more for your money.

Join the O'Reilly Community, and register the O'Reilly books you own. It's free, and you'll get:

- $4.99 ebook upgrade offer
- 40% upgrade offer on O'Reilly print books
- Membership discounts on books and events
- Free lifetime updates to ebooks and videos
- Multiple ebook formats, DRM FREE
- Participation in the O'Reilly community
- Newsletters
- Account management
- 100% Satisfaction Guarantee

Signing up is easy:

1. **Go to: oreilly.com/go/register**
2. **Create an O'Reilly login.**
3. **Provide your address.**
4. **Register your books.**

Note: English-language books only

To order books online:
oreilly.com/store

For questions about products or an order:
orders@oreilly.com

To sign up to get topic-specific email announcements and/or news about upcoming books, conferences, special offers, and new technologies:
elists@oreilly.com

For technical questions about book content:
booktech@oreilly.com

To submit new book proposals to our editors:
proposals@oreilly.com

O'Reilly books are available in multiple DRM-free ebook formats. For more information:
oreilly.com/ebooks

O'REILLY®

Spreading the knowledge of innovators   oreilly.com